METAL CLAY
THE COMPLETE GUIDE

INNOVATIVE TECHNIQUES TO INSPIRE ANY ARTIST
By Jackie Truty

©2007 Jackie Truty
Published by

kp krause publications

An Imprint of F+W Publications

700 East State Street • Iola, WI 54990-0001
715-445-2214 • 888-457-2873
www.krausebooks.com

Our toll-free number to place an order or obtain
a free catalog is (800) 258-0929.

Library of Congress Catalog Number: 2006935443

ISBN: 978-0-89689-430-3

Designed by Rachael Knier
Edited by Susan Sliwicki
Diagrams by Robert Stotts

Printed in China

DEDICATION

To my husband, the paste type of my life, who holds it (and me) together.

ACKNOWLEDGMENTS

First and foremost, to the staff at Art Clay World, USA, Inc., for their patience and support in my physical and mental absences during the writing of this book.

To my daughter, Kate Baum, who lent her beautiful hands and spirit to "the cause."

To the Master and Senior Art Clay Instructors, whose work is included in this book. Their creativity and dedication is always appreciated and admired.

To Susan Sliwicki at Krause Publications, who oversaw this publication through its various editorial permutations.

To Aida Chemical Industries Ltd., for its support in our continuous pursuit of excellence.

Finally, to metal clay artists everywhere who have embarked upon a course, the destination of which has not yet been charted. May our journey be filled with exciting challenges and endless opportunities along the way.

About the Author

Once an operating room nurse and nurse manager, Jackie Truty saw a metal clay demonstration and knew she'd found her niche. Since 2000, she has worked in Art Clay Silver, for which she received her master's training in Japan.

Today, Jackie runs Art Clay World USA as president and owner. She also tours the United States teaching, demonstrating and representing Art Clay. In addition, she appears in the latest Art Clay instructional DVD. She has received international recognition for "Sacred Mountain Guardian," an Art Clay work, at the Silver Accessories Contest in Japan.

Jackie's previous books include "Art Clay Silver and Gold" (Krause Publications, 2003) and "Dichroics: Art Glass All Dressed Up" (Glass Press, 2002).

Jackie lives in the Chicago area with her husband. Visit her Web site at www.artclayworld.com.

TABLE OF CONTENTS

Chapter 1
Past and Present

To know what metal clay is and where it's going, you need to understand its past. And, even though the medium itself is in its infancy, the science that led to its birth has been around for more than a century. But even before that, before humanity developed the concept of "science," knowledge of certain elements in nature existed. These were the elements that made civilization possible.

History

Silver was identified as an element nearly 6,000 years ago, right behind gold and copper. It is the most chemically active of all the noble metals. It is found freely in nature, and ranks second only to gold in malleability and ductility. Silver is harder than gold, but softer than copper. It is one of seven metals known in the ancient world, the others of which are gold, copper, lead, tin, iron and mercury.

Metallurgy is defined as the science and technology of metals, the study of metals in bulk and at their atomic levels. In ancient times, metallurgists focused on learning about metals, their characteristics and how to use them in order to make tools, coins and body adornments.

Smelting, or the process of extracting a metal from its parent ore under controlled conditions, allowed relatively pure forms of silver, gold and iron to be processed.

The smelting of iron and more durable alloys, such as bronze and brass, were discovered and added to the growing list of metals, which replaced the softer silver and gold. However, the brightness, workability and malleability of these two elemental metals, as well as their relative rarity and resistance to oxidation, made them perfect for body adornment and functional art objects.

Aida Chemical Industries

Tradition Vs. New-Age Technology

Metalworking is a broad term that can't begin to be addressed here, even as an overview. There are dozens of techniques that use both hot and cold metal methods, most of which trace their origins back thousands of years.

The only way to even attempt to compare working with metal clay to using traditional methods is to narrow the comparison to those techniques complex enough to warrant its use. For example, using the techniques of chasing and repousse, which involve creating three-dimensional shapes by using punches and hammers on the inside of flat metal (think the Statue of Liberty), wouldn't be an efficient or economical use of fine silver clay.

However, when you think in terms of creating dimensional objects, sculptural forms, engraved and highly detailed forms in silver and gold, then you have the perfect application for the use of metal clay.

With metal clay there is no initial preparation with wax, no sprues, no investment, no burn-out, no melting of metals, no vacuum or centrifugal casting. If you prefer, there's no soldering of any kind. Molding, carving, drying, sanding, firing and polishing metal clay are the only steps involved. What you see in unfired clay is what you get when you are finished, minus the shrinkage rate, which varies from 8-12% depending on metal clay brand. Best of all, everything in metal clay prior to firing is recyclable into more clay and paste, ready for reuse.

That's not to say that mastering metal clay techniques is easy, but the time, money and product investments are far less than those associated with traditional metalworking. And the money is spent in actual product. Aside from the possible (and wholly voluntary) cost of an electric kiln, there are no expensive machines to rent or purchase and no exclusive tools needed to work in metal clay.

SINTERING

Sintering involves creating complex metal designs without fabrication. As early as the 19th century, platinum powders were pressed under heat to create the first sintered compacts. Huge growth in this relatively new industry occurred just after World War II. Sintered metal powders of various types were used to create all kinds of parts for cars, aircraft and machinery.

Sintering technology had come of age. But it wasn't until the early 1990s that Japan became the center of something radically different in sintered

Metal Power Industries

metal technology. For the first time, powdered precious metals were being mass-produced for the express purpose of creating jewelry and other art objects.

The International Organization for Standardization (ISO) defines sintering as "The thermal treatment of a powder or compact at a temperature below the melting point of the main constituent, for the purpose of increasing its strength by bonding together of the particles."

Add water and an organic binder to keep those particles together until sintering is complete and you have — you guessed it — metal clay.

Human history has included 6,000 years of metalworking, nearly 200 years of powder metallurgy, but only a mere 10 years of metal clay. And yet, this relatively new artistic medium has taken root in every inhabited continent, from Asia to North and South America, Europe, Oceania and Africa. Even so, those working in metal clay number only in the thousands. However, thanks to the Internet and today's world of instantaneous communications, the next 10 years will see metal clay blossom and add its unique voice to humanity's long list of artistic expression.

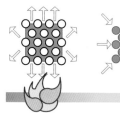

Metal Clay Unveiled

Fine Silver vs. Sterling Silver

In order to understand what metal clay becomes, you have to understand what it is not.

Sterling silver is an alloy. That means it is composed of more than one metal. Other examples of alloys are bronze and brass. Sterling silver typically is comprised of 92.5 percent fine silver and 7.5 percent copper. The copper provides additional strength and hardness. But it also has the unfortunate characteristic of combining with oxygen to create cupric oxide: nasty, black, fire scale. And, it is what causes sterling silver to tarnish more quickly than fine silver.

The Original Clays

All silver metal clays are composed of micron-sized particles of silver, a cellulose-based binder and water. When the dried clay is heated to around 500 F (260 C), the binder burns away, leaving room between the silver particles for consolidation during the sintering process.

Originally, the sintering temperature of metal clay was between 1,600 F and 1,650 F (870 C to 900 C). The particles of silver, between 1 and 20 microns in size, completed the sintering process between 10 minutes and 2 hours, depending on the brand of clay and temperature. This is well below 1,760 F (960 C), the melting point of silver.

There are a few variations of the sintering curve that allow some trade-offs between time and temperature. For example, you can fire the standard form of Art Clay Silver at either 1,600 F (870 C) for 10 minutes, or at 1,472 F (800 C) for 30 minutes. The extended time at the lower temperature allows the curve to reach the same stage of completion.

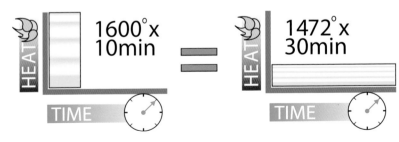

LOWERING THE SINTERING TEMPERATURE

Even an innovation like metal clay can be improved, and it didn't take manufacturers long to discover a way to lower the sintering temperature. There were several reasons why metal clay users were ecstatic about this improvement.

+ Standard metal clay temperatures were too high to fire sterling silver. The copper in the sterling would oxidize, creating fire scale, which weakened the sterling and increased chances of breakage.

+ Standard metal clay temperatures caused any decorative glass inclusions to yellow at the point where they came in contact with the silver. This was the result of a well-known chemical interaction and was, for the most part, unavoidable at these temperatures.

+ Using standard metal clay temperatures meant that only a limited list of colored gemstones could be fired in place.

Within five years of metal clay's appearance, low-fire formulas had appeared. Instead of 1,472 F for 30 minutes, one brand fired at 1,110 F for 30 minutes, while the other fired at 1,200 F for 30 minutes. What this meant was that not only could sterling silver be fired with fine silver metal clay

(increasing the variety of findings that could added), but also that clear glass would not yellow, and a much broader list of colored gemstones could be fired in place. All of these benefits depended on the lower range of firing being used.

With the advantages of using the low-fire metal clays also came some confusion. Being able to sinter at lower temperatures didn't mean that these same low-fire clays couldn't also fire at the standard, higher-firing temperatures,

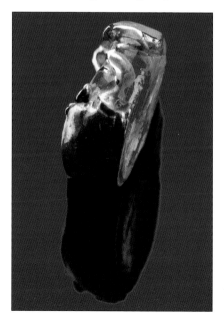

albeit for a shorter amount of time. For instance, you could fire a piece at 1,200 F for 30 minutes, and you also could fire it at 1,472 F for 5 minutes or at 1,600 F for 5 minutes and obtain similar results. There is some evidence that firing at higher temperatures for longer periods of time increases the strength of the resultant fine silver, but those results have been disputed by at least one manufacturer.

One other important thing happened as a result of the introduction of low-fire metal clay. Because the low-fire paste type, which was introduced at the same time as its clay counterpart, could also be fired at the standard temperatures, the standard paste type became immediately obsolete. It was soon discontinued, as were some of the sizes of the standard clay type and the standard syringe type.

Even with the success and advantages of low-fire clays, attempts to totally eliminate standard clays have met with loud, and, so far, successful objection. Most metal clay artisans agree that, due to texture or moisture content, the standard clays continue to have their place as creative options.

SHRINKAGE

All metal clays shrink. It's an inevitable result of the sintering process, as the silver or gold particles bond tightly together. Shrinkage is so predictable, in fact, that it is an irrefutable indicator of the success of sintering. This is especially important when measurable temperature is not present, such as in the use of gas stove top or torch to fire the metal clay. If the final piece has not shrunk to the documented amount, the piece has not been sintered properly, and it must be refired to prevent brittleness and possible breakage.

The actual range of metal clay shrinkage depends on the type and brand used, so it is important to determine this percentage prior to firing. Check the instructions that come with each package. Fortunately, these ranges are quite stable from brand to brand, so predicting the size of a ring or stone bezel is easily done.

OTHER CONSISTENCIES

Aside from the actual moldable, malleable clay, there are other primary consistencies, both available only in the low-fire formula.

Paste Type or Slip

This is basically clay with more moisture. It is akin to slip in ceramic circles. It can be used alone, as a glue to join pre-fired clay pieces together or to repair broken or damaged green ware.

Syringe Type

This type is useful for intricate work, such as work over burnout forms, repair and decoration. A syringe is loaded with 10 g of specially formulated clay.

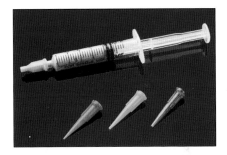

SPECIALTY FORMULAS

A variety of specialty metal clays and pastes are available on the market. Following is a list of the formulas that Art Clay has developed.

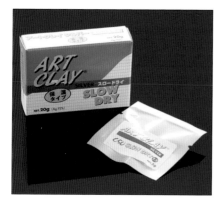

Slow Dry Clays

Created both in standard and low-fire formulas, Slow Dry clay has binders that allow the user to work for a longer time before drying. Stable enough to extrude through an empty syringe, Slow Dry clays can be woven, braided and twisted into limitless designs. They are perfect for small, thin or delicate applications.

Paper (sheet) Type

In a class all its own, paper-type clay looks and feels like a square of vinyl. It has almost no moisture whatsoever, and it can be used in several ways:

+ Alone, folded into fan-like or origami shapes, as was originally intended in Japan.

+ Punched and cut into shapes for use as appliqué on green ware.

+ In strips for rings and as a substitute for bezel wire.

Paper type must be used with as little moisture as possible, and its pristine surface is easily destroyed by even a drop of paste type or water. Conversely, additional heat will cause it to become brittle and break. It must be fired at 1,472 F for 30 minutes.

Oil Paste

The only metal clay formula that is not water-soluble, Oil Paste was created specifically to bond fired silver to fired silver. Applications include repairing cracks or breaks in fired pieces, sealing seams in pre-made fine silver bezel wire, and adding silver to silver. It requires a solvent to thin it and to clean brushes.

Gold Paste

While Gold Paste must be fired at 1,472 F (800 C), like Silver Overlay Paste, it can fire directly to ceramics and glass, as well as fired silver. Although water-soluble, it includes a special dilutant to use with nonsilver applications.

Gold Clay

Gold clays are still evolving, though their exorbitant prices make them used only rarely in solid form. Except for one brand's formula, which can be fired at the same temperature as silver clay, gold clays fire in the range of 1,800 F (982 C). Instead, they often are diluted with water into a paste, which is painted onto silver clay green ware.

When torch fired, the gold bonds to the silver much like keum boo, the Korean technique that bonds gold foil to hot silver.

Silver Overlay Paste

A low-fire product, Silver Overlay Paste fires permanently to nonporous surfaces, such as ceramics, glass and certain gemstones. It is water-soluble and can be used as a substitute for Oil Paste on projects that need low-fire series temperatures.

Chapter 2
Materials and Tools

One of the many advantages of working with metal clay is the lack of specialized equipment necessary to work with it. Most items can be found around the home, studio or garage. The monetary investment is made in product, not expensive tools that may not be used or may become obsolete in 10 years. That said, I admit I have containers of rollers, stamps, brushes and various other items I've taken from my kitchen and never returned because they were essential to my metal clay work. After all, there are priorities!

ROLLING

Theoretically, you can use anything to roll out metal clay, as long as you've treated it so the clay won't stick. Rolling the clay serves either to flatten it or to add texture to it. Either way, you want to use something about 1" in diameter so it rolls evenly. The two most common materials for rollers are acrylic and polyvinyl chloride, also known as PVC, which is commonly used in plumbing pipes.

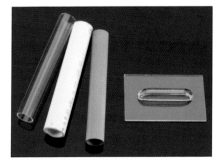

WORK SURFACES

Depending on how you're going to dry metal clay, you want a work surface that is mobile. There's nothing more frustrating than trying to lift a wet metal clay piece from a desktop without damaging it. Originally, the surface of choice was baking parchment. But parchment tended to curl when wet, and sometimes, delicate metal clay pieces would break when an artist would attempt to remove them from the parchment.

Other popular work surfaces are glass, plastic sheet protectors commonly found at office supply stores and nonstick work surfaces. My personal choice is the thin, nonstick surface. It holds up well under the heat of drying boxes, dehydrators and griddles. The clay slides right off when it is dry, and the surface is fairly indestructible (except for that pesky craft knife).

DETERMINING THICKNESS

The rule of thumb is that for a flat metal clay piece to be structurally sound, it should be a minimum of 1 mm thick. Of course, there are circumstances when you would want to roll out thicker or thinner clay. For example, you might want your clay thicker if you were going to stamp it or press flat bezel wire into it. There are a wide variety of methods to achieve your desired thickness. Standard matt board, the kind used around pictures, is approximately 1 mm thick. However, matt board has some give to it, and pressing down hard on your roller can cause the metal clay to be thinner than the minimum 1 mm.

Other measuring devices are playing cards, which can be taped together in pairs. You'll see thicknesses referred to as "3-card" or "5-card" thicknesses. How thick this is, however, depends on the thickness of your cards. The majority of playing cards are a standard thickness, but variations do exist.

There also are plastic strips made exclusively for use with metal clay. The strips come in sets that are just 1 mm thick and color-coded sets that include multiple thicknesses. To use a strip, place it on your work surface, and place the roller across the strip. The slats prevent the metal clay from getting any thinner than you want.

CUTTING

One of the wonderful characteristics of metal clay is that it's soft until it dries. That makes it easy to cut.

When it comes to cutting tools for metal clay, anything with an edge will do. The same tools used to cut polymer clay work well for metal clay. From long, tissue blades (originally used by surgeons to harvest skin tissue), to metal clay fids, to clay and cookie cutters, to metal spatulas with narrow edges, anything and everything in between will do the job. Of course, traditional, razor-edged craft knives also will work, especially if you have to cut a particular pattern or follow a template.

FORMING

Another incredible metal clay characteristic is its ability to take a shape — ANY shape. Into, onto, over, under, around and through, metal clay does it all. Extrude it through a syringe or a polymer clay or cookie gun. Push it into a mold made for butter, or from an old button or a mold carved from soap. Drape clay or brush paste type over molds made from cork clay, bread or pasta. If it can burn out, you can use it. To be absolutely sure your chosen material can burn out, test any material you haven't used previously before you begin your piece. Paper clay is a perfect example of why you want to test

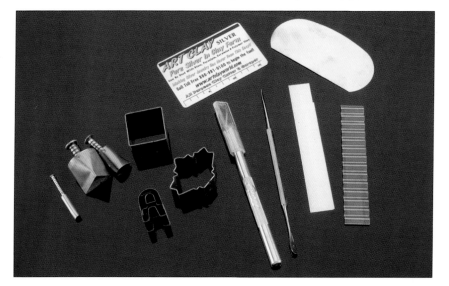

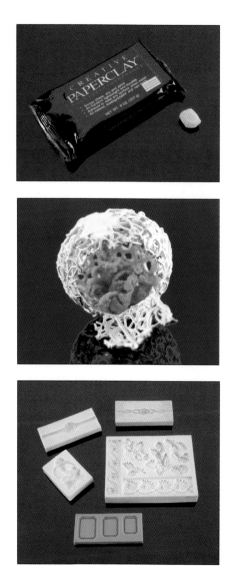

burnout materials. Though paper clay looks like it would burn out completely, it actually doesn't, and it would leave a hardened mess inside of a bead you thought would be hollow.

Speaking of cork clay, you won't (in my humble opinion) find a better molding material around which to form metal clay. It's thoroughly malleable, and, after it's completely dry, cork clay can be filed, carved and sanded to any shape. Best of all, it's totally nontoxic and burns completely, leaving a dried ash that rinses away.

As for ready-made molds into which to push wet metal clay, there are a number of sources. Flexible molds made for polymer clay work well and are more realistically sized than others, such as those for soap. Molds made from silicone lend themselves to metal clay and, for those traditionalists, also will tolerate hot wax. Some molds are flexible enough to allow the clay to be popped out while it is still damp; others are not. In those instances, dry the clay in the mold, and then turn it over to release the piece.

Of course, there are molding materials available that will allow you to create molds of your own, whether from found objects or previously made metal clay pieces. The actual techniques will be covered in a later chapter, but some examples include two-part silicone molding materials, certain plasters and temporary molding materials, such as "Oyumaru," which softens with hot water and hardens when cooled.

Forming also includes propping. Until metal clay dries, it's subject to the laws of gravity. To defy gravity, you can use straws, toothpicks, fiber blanket or anything else at hand.

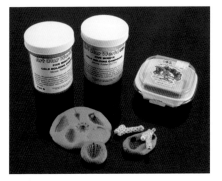

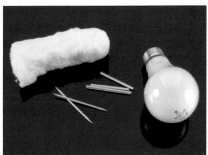

 DANGER: DO NOT use ANY plastics, including the plastic foam commonly known as Styrofoam, as core materials that need to be fired. These plastics produce toxic fumes that can be harmful to you, your family and other living things.

Drying

Before we became an instant society, back when travel times were measured in hours and days, not mere minutes, we would have allowed our metal clay pieces to air dry. Depending on the part of the world you lived in, that might take many minutes to many hours.

We are an instant society, however, and we are constantly on the lookout for shortcuts to dry metal clay. The trick is to apply heat without altering the organic binders. If you apply too much heat, the binders will begin to burn off, which will render the piece brittle and unalterable.

A hair blower/dryer and cardboard box were my first choice of drying tools, until I discovered the food dehydrator. Also adequate are mug warmers, pancake griddles, toaster ovens and food warmers, though these are better suited for flat pieces. You may also place pieces in a kitchen oven, although it is strongly suggested you first test the oven with an oven thermometer to avoid the "Fahrenheit 451" syndrome (the temperature of which Ray Bradbury wrote in his cautionary tale at which paper burns).

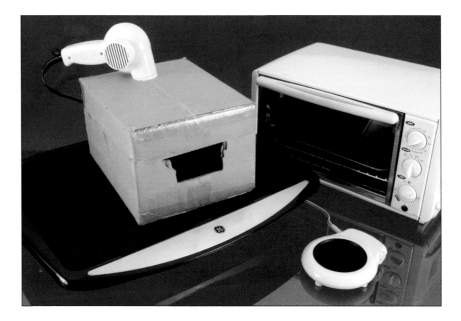

PRE-FIRING

Before sintering, all of the dried bits that are sanded, carved and filed off of the piece are recyclable with water. The manual tools used to do the sanding, carving and filing are found in just about every room of the house, studio and garage, including: clay carving tools made of wood, plastic and metal; various files in cuts from coarse to extra fine; and dozens of different grits of sandpapers and sanding discs.

Electric power-driven rotary tools, such as those sold under the brand names of Dremel and Proxxon, also work. For those who desire the ultimate power tool (no, not a reciprocating saw) there is a water- or oil-cooled, compressor-assisted, ultra-turbine drill/carver. One brand name is Powercrafter. Some consider this Ferrari of hand tools a bit over the top, but with zero vibration and enough revolutions per minute (400,000 rpm) to carve steel like butter, it's the absolute final word in metal clay-shaping decadence.

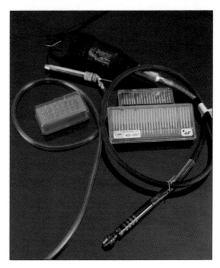

FIRING

Fortunately for us, sintering metal clay doesn't require the degree of heat and temperatures needed to sinter industrial metals. Any number of firing methods can be accommodated between 1,200 F to 1,600 F (650 C to 870 C). Even gold clay doesn't have firing temperatures so high as to make sintering it unavailable to most of us.

The three most common methods of firing are the torch, the gas stove top and the electric kiln. Each method has its advantages and disadvantages.

Some other firing methods are more ingenious, and they have given us a wider variety to choose from, depending on the circumstances. These include the Speedfire Cone System and the Ceramic Hot Pot. Again, there are pros and cons for each, not the least of which are safety considerations.

No matter which firing method you choose, it is essential to precisely follow the instructions for complete and total sintering. There is only so much leeway the sintering curve will allow before something has to "give."

In all circumstances except the electric kiln, the color of the metal will determine the appropriate sintering temperature.

For this reason there is no one kind of gas or torch — acetylene, butane, propane or MAPP gas — that is "better" than another. We're speaking of sintering the metal here, not safety features of individual torches. Whether your torch is made for soldering, glass bead making or welding, if you keep your eyes on the

metal and hold at the appropriate color, you'll fire successfully.

As far as gas stoves are concerned, it makes no difference whether it's natural or bottled gas that fuels it. The only caveat is that it must have enough British Ter (the measure of heat known as British thermal units) for the piece to achieve sintering.

Other materials and tools used in firing are: heat-resistant tongs, tweezers and gloves; prop materials, such as fiber blanket and vermiculite; and firing surfaces, such as stainless steel net, fiber board, fiber paper and ceramic shelves. In the case of less-precise methods, such as gas stove top and torch firing, a digital timer is invaluable.

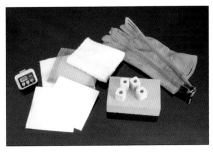

POLISHING

After firing, most of the same tools and materials used on the clay will work on the silver, though polishing fired silver takes substantially more effort.

A stainless steel or brass brush will result in a matte or satin finish. Using wet to dry sandpapers in 600, 1,200 and 2,000 grit will result in a high polish. Innumerable manufacturers have variations on the traditional sandpapers, including sanding pads and sticks, color-coded polishing cloths, etc. All achieve varying levels of polish.

A rotary, vibratory or magnetic tumbler, used in conjunction with stainless steel shot, water and some kind of nonammoniated cleaner, will shine fired silver wonderfully, but it won't smooth the surface. That needs to be done prior to firing.

Burnishers are another way to polish small or large surface areas. The most popular types are metal and agate. Both have highly polished heads and are used to compress the top layer of silver, which results in a less porous, very reflective surface.

Lastly, there are a myriad of rotary power tools with adaptors for surface polishing, including discs, brushes, pins, etc.

The Contenti Company

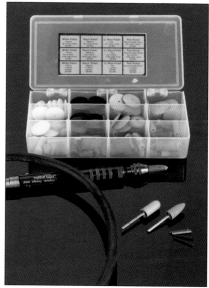

The Contenti Company

Chapter 3
Metal Clay Care
and Handling

There are some basic concepts used throughout the metal clay creative process. Some might call them "tips." I prefer to call them "points of experience." In either case, this basic information will be indispensable to you as you begin your metal clay journey.

Keeping Clay Moist

Every time you pause to talk to someone, look at (or for) something, or simply examine the state of your work, air can steal precious moisture from your open clay. There are a host of methods used to delay the inevitable cracking and drying.

One of the very first measures to take is to use a barrier between your clay, and the dryness of your hands. Most popular are olive oil and products like Badger or Bag Balm.

Place your clay between or under plastic wrap. Preventing the air from reaching the clay and maintaining the moisture is a basic solution.

The downside is that it's tough to shape and mold the clay this way. But it's a simple solution while kneading and rolling out flat shapes.

Place a damp paper towel on your piece during resting moments. This provides much-needed moisture while keeping the air out.

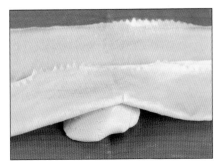

Spray a fine mist of water on your clay from time to time. Don't use a regular household spray bottle, as the droplets are too large. A small, plastic atomizer, like the kind used for perfumes, works best.

Keep an electric humidifier running in your work space. There are many models used to add moisture to the air, and a small unit within a couple of feet of your space can work wonders.

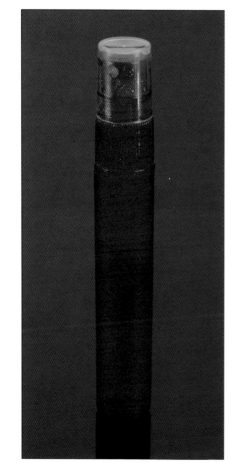

Some people add a drop of glycerin to the clay itself, which provides an internal barrier between the clay and the air. The danger is that adding too much can alter the characteristics of the clay.

Using a Slow Dry clay formula is also a solution. The Slow Dry brand of clay is made specifically to extend the working time before drying up to four to five times beyond that of standard clay. This allows you to do fine detail work, including shaping and braiding, without adding more water. The only down side is that it takes longer to dry the clay completely. Check the Appendices for drying times.

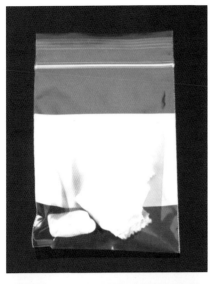

I'm frequently asked how long Slow Dry clay takes to dry, and, when I respond four to five times longer, the next question invariably is, "Well, how long is that?" My answer is, "If you live in Miami, it's a whole lot longer than if you live in Las Vegas." Every climate has a different effect on the clay. If it takes normal clay 5 minutes to dry, it will take around 20 minutes for Slow Dry clay. If it dries immediately upon opening the package — I watched it happen before my eyes while teaching in the Nevada desert — you've only got 5 minutes to get the most out of your clay before those evil cracks appear.

Storing your opened clay can be a real challenge. The better you protect the clay from the air, the longer it will stay moist. Here are some suggestions to achieve that:

• Wrap your clay in plastic wrap, and place your clay in a resealable plastic bag.

• Add a moist sponge, a moist paper towel or a few drops of water to the bag to maintain moisture levels.

• Purchase a jar with a screw-on lid, and store your clay that way. The best jar that I've seen is a small cosmetics jar, which has an inner screen that holds a small sponge. The damp sponge is separated from the actual clay, so it doesn't get muddy. This really keeps the clay moist.

Reviving Dried-Out Clay

Should your clay dry out, don't despair. With a little patience, you can rehydrate it to its former usability.

1 Put the hard piece in a resealable bag, along with several drops of water and a damp paper towel. Seal the bag well, and let it sit for an hour or so.

2 Begin to knead the clay while it is still in the bag, and work the water in.

3 Add more water by the drop if it is needed, but with a little time, the clay will soften again to workability.

Recycling Clay

Recycling clay can be tricky if you regularly use more than one type of clay. Different formulas have different binders, and the manufacturers don't recommend mixing them. For example, if you have a large amount of Slow Dry formula, don't mix it with the regular clay.

Any dried clay filings can go into your paste jar, provided that they are the same formula.

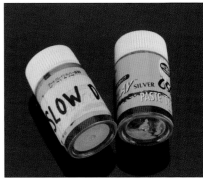

If you still use a standard clay that isn't a low-fire formula, you have to be very careful where you put your leftovers. If you have a paste jar that has clay that can fire at 1,200 F, you don't want to add clay that can only fire at 1,472 F or higher. If you do mix leftover clays, you have effectively contaminated that entire jar, and you must fire all the slip and pieces using that slip at the higher temperature!

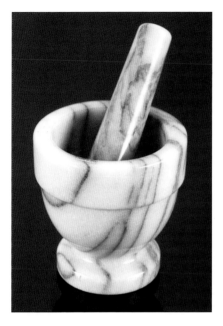

If you have a jar of standard slip made from clay that fires at a higher temperature, you can add any bits of dried clay, whether they are high-fire or low-fire types. It makes no difference, because the low-fire clay can be fired at the higher temperature without adverse effects.

The opposite, however, is not true. If you fire standard, higher-firing clay at lower temperatures, it won't sinter properly, and it will be brittle after firing.

Your best bet is to label your jars and bags; markers work well. And, if you can't remember what you put in the jar, consider it a high-fire jar.

When recycling clay, I've found that a good, old-fashioned mortar and pestle (the kind that pharmacists and cooks use to grind ingredients) works really well on dried bits.

If you don't grind them first, it will take a long time for them to soften in the existing paste, and your slip will be lumpy. I've heard of people using dedicated electric coffee grinders, but I've never used one myself. Just make sure that whatever tool you use, it is dedicated to metal clay. There's nothing worse than finding pieces of silver clay in your ground coffee!

The Hows and Whys of Drying

Before you can fire metal clay, it must be bone dry. That means no moisture can remain in the clay. There is nothing worse than having a piece that explodes or pops in the kiln because the excess moisture has turned to steam, which in turn has turned to energy and made its escape through the front or back of your piece.

I refer to these little bursts as my "Alien" babies, since they remind me of the newborn's method of exit in the movie of the same name.

You wouldn't think that how you dry your metal clay would be important, but you'd be surprised how important it is. How hot and how fast you dry clay has a real effect on the result.

DRYING METHODS

There are three basic ways to dry metal clay: naturally, by heat alone or by a combination of air and heat.

Depending on where you live, it might take several minutes to several hours to air-dry your piece. If you're not in a rush, this is a no brainer.

If you dry a piece by heat alone, such as with an oven or toaster oven, the heat surrounds the piece. But with griddles, cup warmers and the like, the heat is from a specific source. The metal clay piece will dry first where the heat touches it, and then the remainder of the piece will dry by conduction. If it is heated too quickly, the piece will distort, as some parts dry faster than others.

The third and, in my opinion, the best method, is by a combination of air and heat, such as convection ovens, hair dryers and food dehydrators. Of the methods that combine air and heat, my absolute favorite is the food dehydrator.

There are a variety of advantages:

- Dehydrators are made to run for days, even weeks.

- They last virtually forever.

- They are relatively quiet, and they won't disrupt classes or creativity.

- The temperature can be regulated.

- The shelves can, for the most part, be removed to allow for large items, such as ring mandrels.

My second choice is the convection oven. The oven's air currents more evenly dry the piece. Plus, you can regulate the temperature.

My least-favorite drying method is the hair dryer. For one, it's very noisy. Secondly, they tend to be very hot, and they may heat the outside of the piece more quickly than the middle. Generally, there is no thermostat to regulate temperature, other than the "low" and "high" settings.

Whatever method you use to hasten drying, I believe the best way to avoid distortion or warping is to use the lowest temperature possible.

How to Tell if a Piece is Dry

How can you tell when the piece is dry? Actually, it's pretty simple.

Get a flat piece of glass, acrylic or metal. Place the piece directly from the griddle, dehydrator or oven onto the flat surface.

Count to 15 (one-one thousand, two-one thousand, etc.) and remove the piece. If there is a cloud of condensation left behind, you can be sure there's still moisture inside the piece.

Resume drying the piece with your method of choice. Dry the piece for several more minutes, and repeat the process.

FILING AND SANDING SUCCESS

By far, the most green ware breakage happens during the filing and sanding stage. Most of the time, it's not the hand with the tool in it that causes the damage: It's the hand that's holding the piece. We're anxious, intent and focused on our pieces. And, while we're being careful not to exert too much pressure on the file, all of that tightly contained energy is flowing into our nondominant hand.

The first step toward keeping a piece intact is to use a rubber block. The block is a 2" x 2" square of formed, recycled rubber. It is waterproof, it has a little give to it, and it gives you a wide range of filing and sanding options. It's amazing what raising your piece 2" off of the table surface will do for convenience.

Whether you hold a file in your right hand or your left hand, it's the nondominant hand you must watch. Holding and supporting a piece correctly during filing and sanding is the key to keeping a piece... well, in one piece.

Filing Do's and Don'ts

+ Don't press the piece in the middle when filing. It's a sure-fire way to crack the piece. Hold it on the outside edges.

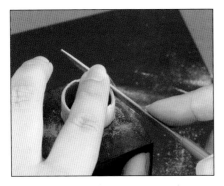

+ Don't put too much stress on your green ware. File exactly where you want, with the least amount exposed, whether you're holding the piece or resting it on a rubber block. The more support you give your piece, the better off you are.

+ Do tap your files often to clear the teeth of clay and dust. The better your file cuts, the less pressure you have to exert on a piece.

+ Do hold your file correctly. File evenly from side to side or on a diagonal.

+ Don't saw back and forth when filing. That motion will result in gouges.

- Do use the right-size file for the job.

- Do use a round file whenever possible, and file side to side. Flat files often leave gouges.

- Don't hold green ware rings only on the outside; that will result in your ring being in four or more pieces. Put a finger on the inside of the ring as counter-pressure when filing or sanding.

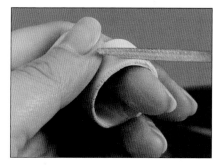

- Do sand your ring on your rubber block. A great way of sanding is to put sandpaper on the block, and rub your ring over the sandpaper. But don't hold your ring on the outside and sand. Place two or three fingers on top of the ring, and sand lightly in circles. Check your progress often.

- Do look more than you sand or file. You can always take off a little more, but it's much harder to put clay back on after you've taken it off.

Firing Options

When deciding how to fire a piece, you need to look at the weakest link. That's rarely the metal clay. Usually, it's whatever (if anything) is being fired with it, such as glass, ceramics, gemstones, etc.

Here are my choices, in order from my favorite to least favorite.

Programmable Electric Kiln

Yes, a programmable electric kiln is the most expensive choice. But it also is the most accurate and most versatile choice. Metal clay artists often create in other media. The programmable kiln, if chosen carefully, can fulfill every need. It can fire glass, ceramics and gemstones. It can anneal glass beads.

An electric kiln that's not programmable (i.e. one without a knob to control temperature) is also a viable alternative, but it must have a babysitter. These kilns don't turn off after the appropriate hold time, and it is not as accurate as a computer-controlled kiln.

Speedfire Cone System

This relatively new option uses a combination of a small or standard propane gas cylinder, an attachable burner, and ceramic cone with a round, metal grate that sits on top. There is a thermocouple, which is used to measure the temperature, inset in the ceramic cone.

The temperature is regulated through the propane leading to the burner, like a gas stove. The ceramic cone concentrates the heat to the grate above and turns it into a miniature stove that can be monitored visually.

Firing glass and ceramics takes a little experience, and you are cautioned against firing cork clay and other organics, although I know many do. The area available on the grate is only several square inches, but the ability to control the temperature makes this system a viable option.

Gas Torch

Theoretically, any gas torch can be used. The torch-firing process focuses on the color of the metal as an indicator of sintering, not only on the distance from the object or the firing time.

While any kind of metal clay or heat-appropriate gemstones can be torch fired, firing metal clay in conjunction with glass, ceramics or organics is not recommended. In addition, there are size and volume restrictions.

While torch firing is one of the least-expensive methods of sintering metal clay, it also is one of the least verifiable. It depends on visual cues to ensure proper firing, and any number of variables can affect its success.

Peacock Industries

Ceramic Hot Pot

This method has the most limitations, and it would be my last choice for firing metal clay. The fuel is a gel, which is measured into a cup at the bottom of the pot. Pieces are placed on the grate, and the gel is ignited.

Only low-fire metal clays can be fired with this method, and there are no controls to monitor the color, extent or degree of firing. Like the torch, size and volume restrictions apply when using the ceramic hot pot.

 DANGER: Except for the programmable kiln, all methods used to fire metal clay require careful monitoring and continued presence. Never leave any of these devices unattended while in use. Keep children away while these devices are in use and until they cool, as they will remain hot for a long time.

Cooling do's and Don'ts

+ Do allow metal clay pieces to cool to room temperature before removing from the kiln, whenever possible.

+ Do make sure to use long tweezers and a heat-appropriate glove when using a kiln.

+ Do have adequate ventilation in your work area during and after the firing process.

+ Don't open a kiln containing metal clay and glass or ceramics until room temperature — not even to peek!

+ Don't quench (dip into cool water) a piece directly from the kiln. Remove the shelf to a heat-safe surface for a minute or two.

+ Never quench pieces that contain gemstones, regardless if they are natural or synthetic. The sudden shock will cause fractures.

+ Don't quench metal clay pieces that have delicate joints or many different thicknesses in their layers. Quenching puts additional stress on the metal and joints, and it can cause fractures.

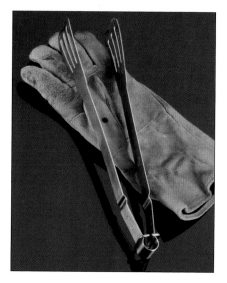

From Matte to Mirror: Choosing Your Finish

It astonishes me how often metal clay artists choose to bury their pieces in dark patinas that mimic lead, pewter and hematite. I have and always will believe that silver should look, whenever possible, like silver.

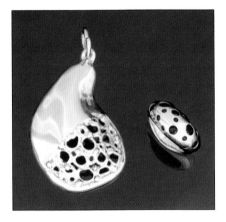

Whether you decide on a matte, satin or mirror finish, there are ways to show off metal clay pieces without making them look like they've been buried since the Middle Ages. If you want your pieces to look thousands of years old, you might choose to imitate the art found in Egyptian tombs rather than English bogs.

I think that part of our confusion is that we inherently know that the silver looks flat without some kind of contrast. In addition to darkening our pieces with liver of sulfur or various acids, however, we also should learn to use design aspects to enhance the visual contrast of our metal clay pieces.

Smooth Vs. Rough

Use the contrast of texture to give your piece dimensionality.

Flat Vs. Curved

Adding height, layering and twists in your design will give your piece a dynamic look.

Matte Vs. Shiny

Instead of throwing the entire piece into the tumbler, use a burnisher to highlight portions of the piece to provide the eye a contrast between shiny and not shiny.

If you're determined to use patinas, learn to use them correctly. For more information on patinas, see Chapter 9.

CHAPTER 4
TECHNIQUES

Techniques are ways to achieve particular results. There may be more than one technique to reach a particular end, and we'll try to include as many as humanly possible. The techniques included in this book are starting points and suggestions. You may prefer one over another, or you may have developed an entirely different technique. There is no "wrong" way to reach your goal.

ROLLING

Rolling out clay seems to be such a basic technique that it should need no explanation. But there are tips to perform even this simple procedure.

Whether you're using a piece of PVC pipe or an acrylic roller, a nonstick work surface or a baking sheet, making metal clay into a very flat sheet takes a little experience. Most people want to exert way too much pressure on the roller and press the clay so hard into the work surface that it becomes attached and can't be removed. This is true even with nonstick surfaces.

So, what's the proper way to roll metal clay? Gently and slowly. Lift and turn the piece 90 degrees every couple of rolls.

Remember, the goal is to get the piece to the dryer as quickly as possible.

This technique serves two purposes: It keeps the piece from sticking to the work surface and makes it easier to roll the piece to an even thickness.

And, don't roll just in the middle of the piece. That creates a thin center and thicker edges — not a flat piece. Flat means flat, not almost flat or mostly flat.

TEXTURING

FOUND OBJECTS

Unlike rubber stamps and plates that are made for the express purpose of creating an image, numerous objects intended for other purposes have found their way into metal clay.

Old buttons can become instant stamps. Or, you can make molds of them so the designs can be reproduced.

Lace, both natural and synthetic, can be rolled and impressed into the clay for wonderful effects.

EVERYDAY OBJECTS

Almost anything, including textured glass, textiles, pressed papers, snakeskin and flooring pieces can create texture. The fact is, metal clay is so readily impressed that even your finger becomes a texture plate. Fingerprints are distinctive and royalty free!

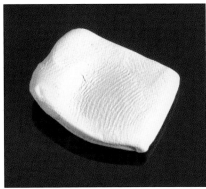

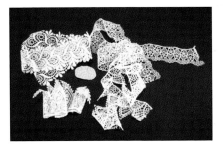

Also, lace made from natural fibers, like silk and cotton, can be coated with layers of slip and fired right in place on a piece.

Leaves and other organic materials, such as fresh and dried pods, are perfect to coat with metal clay, slip and syringe-type clay. Leaves with deep veining can be rolled into the clay as well, and either be removed or left in place and fired out.

MANUFACTURED RUBBER STAMPS AND TEXTURE PLATES

Rubber stamps and texture plates were some of the first textures achieved on metal clay. There are thousands and thousands of different images and textures — some simple, some incredibly complex.

Metal clay can be impressed by or rolled over stamps or plates, which can be made of brass, plastic, silicone, rubber or carved wood. Practice using stamps or plates with some polymer clay to gauge the pressure needed to make a satisfactory impression.

1 Prime the surface of the stamp or plate with some kind of release, such as olive oil or silicone spray, so the clay doesn't stick to the minute details.

2 Press the stamp or plate firmly into the clay, but not so firmly that the surface of the clay is broken. If it's too thin, firing will cause the surface to crack.

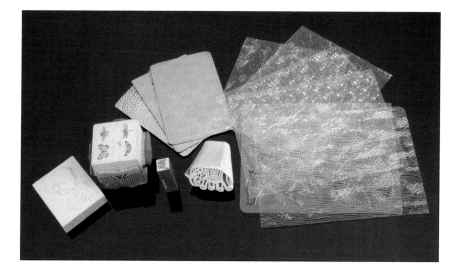

Making Your Own Stamps and Plates

One of the downsides of purchasing ready-made stamps and plates is that thousands of other people have purchased the same designs. Also, many purchased stamps have legal caveats about duplicating the designs for sale.

One solution is to create your own designs, based on royalty-free images. These include historical data from museums, online sites and art sites. I've even downloaded beautiful calligraphy from historical letters found on eBay!

Carving

You can roll metal clay over primed plates that you have carved to achieve unique, royalty-free designs.

Three of the easiest surfaces to carve are readily available. Polymer clay, when baked, makes a terrific surface.

Erasers also work well. Speedball makes a blank, pink rubber pad called a SpeedyStamp, which is made especially for carving.

The third choice is a linoleum-like surface also made for carving. One side is green, the other blue, and black is in the middle.

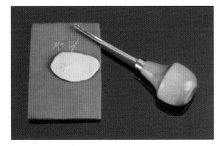

In order to get an even depth, you need to carve through the surface color to the black layer. With just a few linoleum block carving tools, you can create your own carved plates.

Polymer Clay Plates

You also can use polymer clay to make your own plates to be used for what has come to be known as the "tearaway" technique. This involves making a black-and-white copy of any drawing or copyright-free text, then inverting the colors so black becomes the background color. It's important to print the image on heavy card stock; use a photocopier that uses dry toner.

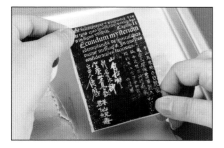

1 Cut the printed card into pieces 2" wide x 3" to 4" long. Lay one piece over a slightly larger sheet of softened polymer clay, which is laid on a metal or glass plate and rolled to the thickest setting on a pasta machine. About ½" of the card's edge should be folded back.

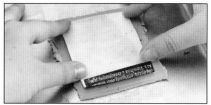

2 Use the side of your hand to vigorously rub the printed card for 2 minutes.

3 Allow the piece to rest 7" to 8" from a regular lamp for 7 minutes.

4 Repeat Steps 2 and 3.

5 After the second resting period ends, hold the tab on the edge of the card stock and use a quick, constant motion to rip it from the bottom polymer clay slice. A thin layer of polymer clay will adhere to the exposed black toner sections.

6 Bake the curled paper and slice of etched polymer clay according to the polymer clay manufacturer's instructions.

7 Oil the stamp well before you use it with metal clay.

Photopolymer Plates

The newest way to create your own, unique stamps and plates with very little effort is a process that uses photopolymer plates. These light-sensitive plates typically are used in the printing industry to make masters for the printing process. They are composed of a backing of metal, polyester or other material onto which a layer of photosensitive polymer is attached.

| Protective cover film (Polyester) |
| Photosensitive nylon resin layer |
| Adhesive & antihalation layer |
| Support base (Polyester film or steel plate) |

Andersen & Vreeland Company

TIP: Protect unexposed plates from sunlight by wrapping them in black plastic.

1 Place a transparency printed with text or pictures over the plate.

2 Expose the plate to ultraviolet light; a halogen light, black light or UV light will work. A halogen light is shown.

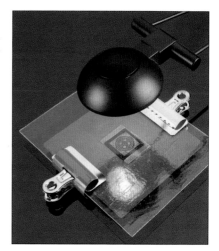

3 After the specified number of minutes (follow the manufacturer's directions), remove the plate from the UV light source and remove the clips and glass.

4 The photopolymer will cure and harden where the surface was exposed to the light through the clear area of the transparency. The area protected from the light by the black, printed part of the transparency will remain soft; scrub it with a nail brush and warm water to wash it away all the way down to the backing.

5 After drying, post-expose the entire plate to cure and harden the remaining areas. Use the same amount of time you used for the first exposure.

6 After exposure and curing, prime the plate with olive oil, and store it with other plates and stamps.

FORMING

MOLDS

Just as nearly anything can be made into a texture plate, just about anything can be made into a mold.

Silicone Molds

Two-part silicone mold mixes are easy to use, and the amount of detail that is picked up is a real bonus. One of my first uses of mold mix was to make a copy of my mother's rhinestone earring. The mold was so perfect that the silicone actually reflected light the way the original earring did!

There are many brands of two-part silicone mold mixes; all work similarly.

1 Knead equal parts of mold mix together into one color.

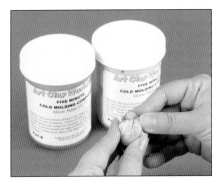

2 Either press the putty around the object to be molded or press the object into the putty.

3 Leave the object and putty together until the putty is cured — usually 5-20 minutes. Pull the object away from the putty. Since the mold is made from silicone-based putty, no release is needed.

Oyumaru

A less-sensitive molding compound comes from Japan. Oyumaru is made for children's modeling. It comes in colorful strips that can be combined for larger pieces. While the detail achieved with Oyumaru isn't nearly as fine as that achieved with the silicone mold mix, it's satisfactory for basic molded shapes.

1 Put the Oyumaru strips into hot water until they are soft.

2 While the compound is hot, you can press anything into it. As the Oyumaru cools, it hardens.

3 To reuse Oyumaru, return it to hot water until the compound softens again.

Organic Forms

Almost anything that is organic and can burn away in the kiln can be used as a form around which to add metal clay, slip or syringe-type clay. The most versatile of these organics is called core cork clay. It's sold as a block of ground cork mixed with water and a binder. It is kept moist, and it must be transferred to a resealable bag once opened. Cork clay can be molded into any shape.

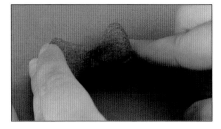

Like metal clay, cork clay must be thoroughly dried before firing. Prior to that, however, it can be filed, carved, sanded and drilled. In the kiln, cork clay is fired at a maximum temperature of 1,472 F. It releases no toxins as it burns cleanly to ash and leaves a hollow, metal clay form.

Other organics include fresh and dried pods, pressed cardboard mini-boxes, pasta, bread, plain crackers and cookies.

Not all organics burn away readily, however. Examples are seashells and paper clay. Seashells have an excess of calcium, which prevents them from burning away. Paper clay leaves a hardened mass, which remains.

If your finished metal clay piece is solid, you may wish to use paper clay and simply let what remains stay inside your piece. If you are creating a hollow form that is transparent, such as a filigree ball or a bead with a cutout design, choose something that completely burns away.

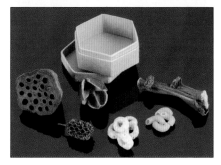

USING SYRINGE TYPE

A pre-filled metal clay syringe contains 10 g of metal clay that can be used in a variety of applications, depending on the nozzle size.

Syringe-type clay is not paste in a syringe, but a special formula with a drier consistency, somewhere between paste and clay. Typically, syringe-type clay comes in one of several packages: with several reusable nozzles with different tip diameters, with just one nozzle or with a refill syringe but no nozzles.

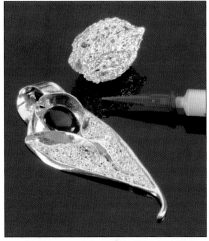

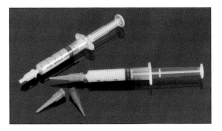

The smallest-diameter nozzle can be used for delicate outlines and decorations and to fill outlines with an open-work, faux filigree.

The medium-diameter nozzle, which is the most common, is used to create gemstone bezels and outlines, to join seams and to fill gaps and cracks.

The largest-diameter nozzle can be used to create stand-alone, decorative elements, such as initials.

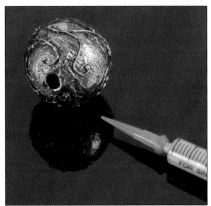

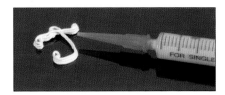

Extruding Metal Clay

By itself, an empty syringe can be used to extrude Slow Dry clay into long ropes, which can be used in several ways.

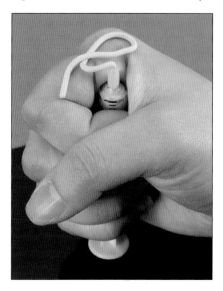

Braiding

With some practice, ropes of extruded Slow Dry clay can be braided for use in rings and other designs.

Bezels

Ropes of Slow Dry clay also can be used as bezels around forms of glass, ceramics and fireable gemstones, such as obsidian and hematite. The shrinkage rate of metal clay actually works to advantage by locking the bezel around the interior form.

TIPS FOR SYRINGE SUCCESS

There are definitely certain techniques needed to create a rounded, beautifully shaped bead of the pre-filled, syringe-type clay. The key secret to successfully using syringe-type clay is keeping the syringed line above the surface of your piece and laying it down exactly where you want it.

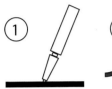 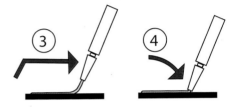

+ Keep the tip of the syringe above the surface. The trick is to extrude slightly ahead of where you need to lay down your line of syringe type. If the nozzle touches the surface, the syringe line will be flattened and unattractive. It takes some coordination to have approximately ½" of syringe-type clay always ahead of your surface, but the goal is to lay the syringe line exactly where you want it.

+ Hold the syringe so that you can see the syringe line as it is extruded. For me, that means gently gripping the barrel of the syringe so my thumb rests on the plunger. You don't need to hold the syringe in a death grip. If you do, your hand will tire very quickly and you'll be exhausted before you're done!

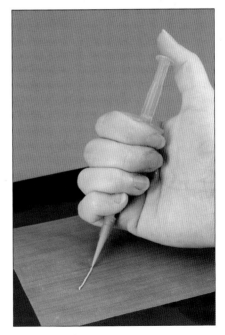

* Always start your syringe line by touching the nozzle to the surface, then lifting it up while pressing the plunger and moving your hand forward. End your syringe line the same way, by touching down and lifting up. The worst thing you can do is end your line by pulling your line into a thin tail and scraping your nozzle on the surface. This not only thins your syringe line, but it can damage your nozzle tip and make it unusable.

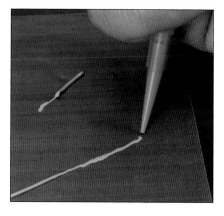

* Support your forearm on the edge of a table, and use your nondominant hand to guide the syringe tip. It's not unusual for your hands to shake a bit when you're concentrating or nervous, and this will definitely help to keep things steady.

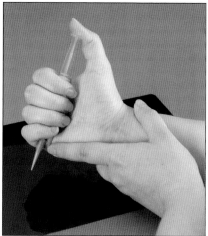

Using Silver Overlay Paste

Sgraffito

Silver Overlay Paste is a specialty metal clay paste formulated to bond to nonporous surfaces, such as glass, glazed ceramics and fireable minerals, such as hematite and obsidian. It is water soluble and can be thinned to apply to nonporous surfaces in a technique known as "sgraffito."

1 Clean the nonporous surface of dirt and oils; alcohol is usually sufficient.

2 Transfer a very small amount of Overlay Paste to a separate container. Add drops of water until the paste is the consistency of skim milk.

3 "Float" a layer of this diluted paste over the surface of the ceramic/glass/obsidian just to the point of translucency. Allow the paste to dry. If the paste is too thin, the silver won't be thick enough, and it will fire dull. If the paste layer is too thick, the design will chip when you try to scratch away the residual paste.

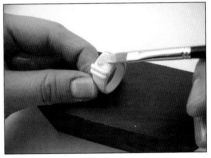

4 Use carbon paper and a toothpick, bamboo skewer or sgraffito tool to transfer a stencil-like design to the surface of the thinned Overlay Paste. If you prefer, you can free-hand the design with a graphite pencil.

5 Use a sgraffito tool, toothpick or bamboo skewer to remove or scratch away the Overlay Paste from unwanted areas. The places where the paste remains will become silver.

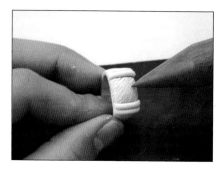

6 Use alcohol on a cotton swab or toothpick tip to remove any stray particles of Overlay Paste. Fire the piece 1,200 F for 30 minutes.

7 Use a metal or agate burnisher to burnish the fired piece. Apply metal polish, and wash the piece with a paste of baking soda and water.

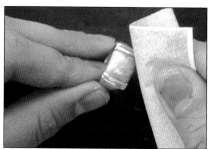

BONDING

Overlay Paste also can act as an intermediary between nonporous surfaces and other types of metal clay to help bond the units.

By putting a primary layer of Overlay Paste on a nonporous surface, any other kind of low-fire clay can be used. This is especially important when small, sculptural elements are applied. Without the first layer of Overlay Paste on these items, these elements would not bond during the firing process.

REPAIRING

With the introduction of low-fire metal clay formulas, there are situations where, after firing, minor repairs are needed. In these circumstances, Oil Paste, which must be fired at 1,472 F for 30 minutes, is inappropriate. Enter Overlay Paste.

Because of its binding characteristics, Overlay Paste makes a perfect repair paste. It can be used full strength, it has a tackier consistency, and it fires as low as 1,200 F for 30 minutes.

USING PAPER TYPE

In Japan, the intended uses for Paper Type clay, also known as Sheet Type clay, seemed very straightforward. It was designed to be folded into origami shapes and to create folded forms for jewelry and home decoration. Outside of Japan, however, we seemed unsure what to do with this square that looked more like vinyl than the metal clay we had come to know.

Paper Type is a 3" x 3" piece of metal clay with nearly all the moisture removed. It has tremendous memory, and it can be folded and creased easily and quickly. Because of its paper-like characteristics, it also can be embossed with metal stamps or even in a typewriter.

However, Paper Type doesn't tolerate moisture. Even a drop of water can destroy and actually dissolve the surface.

Paper Type is best fired by kiln at 1,472 F for 30 minutes, and it can be polished the same as any of the other types of metal clay.

A torch is an acceptable firing method for very small items and clay pieces with Paper Type as appliqué.

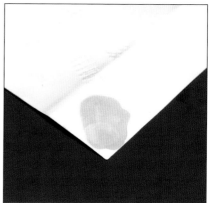

Originally, instructions called for firing Paper Type first, then using Oil Paste to attach findings, etc. As metal clay artists who were unfamiliar with or unable to perform the art of origami became more familiar with Paper Type, they sought their own ways to use it.

APPLIQUÉ

We found that Paper Type was perfect for using with punches and then attaching to unfired metal clay. The challenge was learning how much — or how little — paste type to use to attach appliqués without destroying them.

The answer is simple: Use the absolute least amount possible. All edges of the appliqué must be attached so they don't pull away from the main piece during firing.

If any paste is inadvertently trans- ferred to the surface of the appliqué, it

will alter its characteristics and cause it to look dirty. This can be remedied after firing by sanding.

RING SHANKS AND BEZELS

Paper Type also has been used success- fully to make ring shanks and bezels. However, this method takes a bit more experience, since you can't use paste type with it in any significant amount.

THE FINER POINTS

SEAMS

Seams are where two pieces of metal clay join. These joints are spots of potential weakness, and if they are not solidified and joined properly, seams can be a source of cracking or breaking during or after firing. You must always remember that, when sintering, metal clay shrinks from any edge. A weak seam is a potential edge.

In my opinion, it's absolutely essential to learn to make seams disappear. There's nothing less professional than seeing a seam in a ring shank, in a bezel or in the side of an Inro-type pendant.

One of the significant aspects of firing metal clay is its shrinkage away from edges. Therefore, if there is a gap between two joints, the gap will actually increase during firing — not decrease. The only way to have the entire piece shrink during firing without distorting is to ensure that every seam and joint is solid.

Usually, getting the seam together is not the biggest problem; making it disappear is. Paste and syringe-type clays are used on seams and joints, but we tend to use paintbrushes to level them out prior to firing. Consequently, contraction during drying causes the seam to reappear.

Subsequent filling, filing and sanding occurs over and over in a kind of metal clay purgatory, until the area is weaker than ever.

The solution is to overfill the seam from the very beginning. This way, when you perform your initial filing and sanding, you'll remove the excess clay to the proper level. If in doubt, add more paste or syringe type, and dry thoroughly.

Lids

There are two basic types of lids: fitted and nonfitted. In nonfitted lids, some kind of stop is attached to the inside of the lid to prevent it from falling off.

In fitted lids, the lid actually is created around the top of the main body.

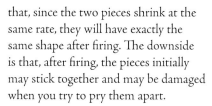

In order for the lid to fit properly after firing, a certain amount of space must be maintained between the lid and the main body. When creating the lid, use a small strip of nonstick work surface around the top of the main body to act as a base for the sides of the lid. In addition, actual firing should seek to minimize distortion of the pieces, so that if the lid fits properly prior to firing, it will fit just as well after firing.

There are two methods to fire the lid. One is to fire it separately from the main body, and the other is to fire it in place. One benefit of firing the lid in place is that, since the two pieces shrink at the same rate, they will have exactly the same shape after firing. The downside is that, after firing, the pieces initially may stick together and may be damaged when you try to pry them apart.

My suggestion is to cut a small strip of fiber paper, the kind used under glass when kiln firing, and place it between the lid and the main body prior to firing.

As the binder burns off and the pieces shrink, this wafer of burnable paper will maintain a small space between the lid and bottom. This will ensure a better fit after the firing is complete.

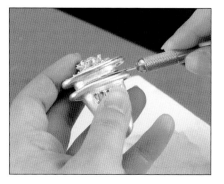

Flowers

Flowers are one of my favorite decorative elements. From calla lilies to roses to gardenias, miniature flowers can be created in fine silver in the same way they are created in the bakery.

Instead of marzipan, though, the medium is Slow Dry clay. Of course, you can use any type of clay, but the flowers and petals are so delicate that using anything other than Slow Dry clay makes cracking and breaking a real problem.

I'm going to illustrate two different kinds of flowers: the rolled rose and the assembled flower, which can be any species that has petals.

Rolled Rose

The rolled rose is perfect for very small accessory flowers. These roses are usually accompanied by a few leaves and they work best in small clusters.

1 Roll out and cut very thin slices of metal clay.

2 Roll the slices, and secure them with a drop of paste type.

3 Create a small pinch at the bottom to give you something to hold onto.

Assembled Flower

The assembled flower takes a bit longer, but is much more natural in appearance.

1 Start with the center bud, or stamen, as the case may be. Roll a tiny amount of clay and fashion a point.

2 Pinch off a small piece of clay, and flatten it with your fingers. Add a drop of paste type to the center stamen, and attach the first petal.

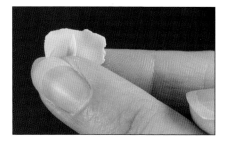

3 Shape the petal as desired.

4 Pinch off another piece and clay and repeat the procedure, attaching the petal in the opposite location.

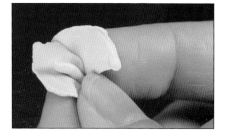

5 Continue to fashion petals and attach them in positions around the center. Connect the petals with drops of paste. Use smoothers and shapers to create dimension and lifelike appearance.

6 Dry the piece thoroughly. You can save these flowers or future use, or you can pre-fire them and attach them at a later time.

Chapter 5
Bails, Loops, Beads and Connectors

The techniques in this chapter address connections made from metal clay used in hanging and attaching. Since fired metal clay is as strong as 18-karat cast gold, connections created and attached with metal clay easily are strong enough for general wear.

Bails

Rollover Bails

A rollover bail uses an extension of the piece's original clay to, just as its name implies, roll over a straw or other mandrel. The other end is then attached to the main piece. There is only one seam, and the bail can go from back to front or from front to back.

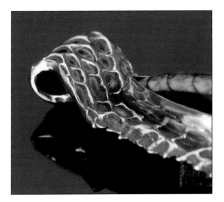

Attached Bails

This kind of bail is separate from the main body of the piece. An attached bail uses the same or different kind of clay, and it can even be made of syringe-type clay. Paste and/or syringe-type clay must be used to connect the bail to the main body.

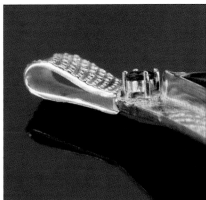

UNBROKEN BAILS

Rather than making a hole in a pendant and inserting a store-bought bail, the unbroken bail technique allows you to create a bail out of metal clay that is fired with the main body but is not attached. The strip or coil of clay is put through the hole, rolled over a mandrel, and then its ends are connected.

The seam is filed and sanded to invisibility. Because no paste or syringe-type clay is used to connect the bail to the main body, the bail won't be permanently attached, and it will rotate freely.

LOOPS

Loops differ from bails only in the direction they lay in relation to the main body of the piece. That is, a bail's hole runs side to side (parallel to the piece), while a loop's hole runs front to back (perpendicular to the piece).

Some loops are made of fine silver wire, some are made of syringe type, and some are made of rolled coils or cut clay.

BUTTON-SHANK LOOP

A variation of the loop is the button-shank loop. This loop is formed much like the loop on a pendant, except it is attached to a button made from metal clay. A straw is normally used as a mandrel, but anything that can be removed or fired in place can be used.

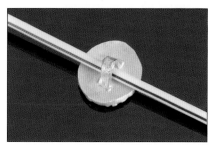

BEAD CAPS

A bead cap hides the end of a strand of beads and caps it, so to speak.

The most common type of bead cap has a hole in it, through which a wire can travel. This wire usually connects to a clasp of some kind.

Cork clay offers the easiest method to create the core for a hollow bead cap. You can shape the cork any way you wish, in any shape you wish.

Cork Clay Base: Wet Method

One benefit of the wet method is that the final bead cap can be fired with a torch or gas stove top. A downside is that delicate or openwork caps might be damaged when you are removing the plastic and cork.

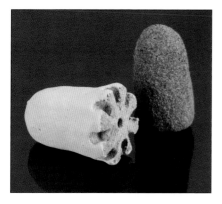

1 Form the cork as desired. Put a straw into the hole to mark it.

2 Poke a hole in a small piece of plastic wrap, and slide it down the straw to the base of the cork.

3 Lay the plastic as flat as possible. Rub a very small amount of olive oil onto the plastic. Cover the plastic in clay, then shape it and let it dry. After drying, gather the plastic. Squeeze the still-moist cork within, then gently pull it out of the green ware bead cap.

4 Return the cap to the dryer.

Cork Clay Base: Dry Method

In the dry method, the cork clay is fully dried before the clay or paste type is applied.

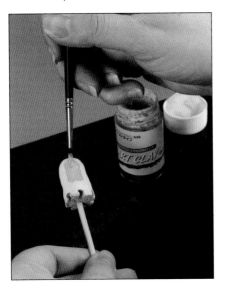

1 Form the cork as desired.

2 Form the bead cap as desired.

3 Fire the entire bead cap, cork included.

Beads

Solid-Formed Beads

A solid-formed bead is exactly what it sounds like: a solid shape of metal clay with a mandrel of some kind. This can take any shape and be decorated any way you like. Mandrels can be plastic straws that are removed prior to firing, or wood or bamboo skewers that burn during firing.

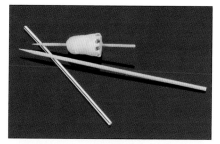

Hollow-Formed Beads

Hollow-formed beads can be formed around cork or other organics. Making them hollow reduces their finished weight. The core can be covered with paste or clay and decorated any way you wish.

Lentil-Shaped Beads

Lentil-shaped beads are dried over forms, such as light bulbs. They are hollow by virtue of their shape when the two sides are combined.

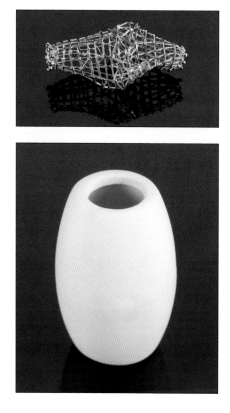

Openwork Hollow Beads

Openwork hollow beads can be formed by using syringe techniques that, after firing, allow light through the metal clay framework. Openwork beads can also be created by cutting holes in the clay prior to drying and firing.

Bisque Ware Beads

There are hundreds of beads available made from fired but unglazed ceramics.

These are called bisque. They are hard, but porous, and they accept paste type readily. They typically are hollow themselves, so putting three coats of paste type on them will produce a silver-coated bisque bead that will use a lot less silver but still have substance.

CONNECTORS

TOGGLES

A toggle is a two-part connector with no moving parts. It works by interlocking its two halves. Toggles can take many shapes and can be made from metal clay simply and easily.

T-bar and circle connectors are among the easiest to design. They can be cut using a paper template. Each half needs a way to connect it to the main necklace or bracelet.

The bar must be wide enough to settle on the circle without falling through, and it must be thick enough (at least 1 mm) to be stable under the weight of the necklace.

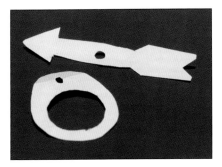

Interlocking Connectors

Interlocking connectors are equally easy to design and make. Two hourglass shapes connect by fitting one into the other and then straightening them out.

This design requires a slight adjustment when you are forming it so that the two pieces fit comfortably together.

Hinges

A hinge is a kind of connector with two halves that rotate around a fixed axis, generally on a single plane. The leaves of the hinge are connected to two different sides. The most common example is a door hinge, though variations can be used on boxes, chests, etc. The pin that goes through the actual tube of the hinge can be permanent or removable.

There are many ways to create metal clay hinges, depending on what size you need, how they'll be used, etc. Although solder could be used to create some or all aspects of a hinge, the following two techniques use no solder at all: one for a small box, the other for a mini-book.

Box Tube and Pin Hinge

I used this method for years when I was creating stained glass boxes. It lent itself well to soldering the pin inside the box seams. In adapting this for metal clay, the design was altered slightly to allow the bent pin to be incorporated into the sides of the box and fired in place.

1 Make a 30 mm x 30 mm template. You will use this for the front and bottom.

2 Cut a 5 mm x 5 mm notch in facing corners of another 30 mm x 30 mm square to use for the two sides.

3 Cut a 30 mm x 26 mm template for the back piece. Measure and cut one 32 mm x 30 mm template for the lid.

4 Cut a 5 mm x 10 mm notch on each opposite side of the lid to create a 20 mm x 10 mm tab.

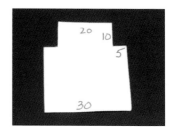

5 Form the tab created in Step 4 around a 20 mm length of brass tube, through which the brass wire will rotate. All of the sides can be cut and dried first, and assembled at the end.

6 Slide a 60 mm length of brass wire through the 20 mm brass tube. Equally bend the pin on each side by 90 degrees to form a "U" shape.

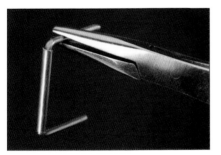

7 Secure the 20 mm tube, formed by the tab of metal clay rolling over the tube, with syringe-type clay. It's important that this tube lay flat and even with the lid, and that the pin move very freely within the tube.

8 When everything is dry, use syringe- and paste-type clays to assemble the six pieces. Bury the bent pin legs in the corners where the two sides join the back.

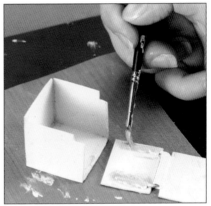

9 Fire at 1,300 F for 30 minutes. Check to make sure the lid rotates freely around the pin.

10 Brush and polish as desired.

Mini-Book Butt Hinge

1 Measure the width of the sides needed for the hinge, and divide that into three equal parts. The two outer parts will go on one side, and the middle section will go on the other side.

2 Take a coffee stirrer and a straight, round wire that fits comfortably inside. Use the stirrer as a mandrel to create three tubes.

3 Roll the clay around the stirrer. Cut through the wet clay at the pre-measured marks.

4 Make sure that the seams are sealed tightly, and let the piece dry.

5 Create the two sides, or flanges, out of clay. Attach the two outer tubes to one side and the middle tube to the other side.

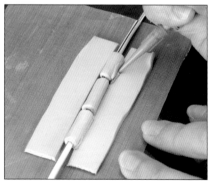

6 Dry the pieces well. Remove the coffee stirrer, and fire the pieces. Heat one end of the wire with a small torch so it forms a ball.

7 Place the wire in a vise, and use a small, ball-peen hammer to flatten the ball.

8 Thread the wire through all three tubes. The amount of wire above the end of the tube should be half of the diameter of your tube. For example, if the tube is 2 mm wide, the visible wire should be 1 mm.

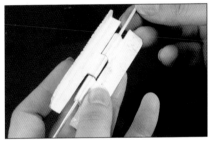

9 Place the piece in a vise or rest it on a metal surface and repeat the procedure for the other end.

10 Make sure the sides of the book rotate freely around the hinge pin.

CHAPTER 6
RINGS, STONES AND FINDINGS

Techniques involving rings, stones and findings are among the most popular. This chapter addresses all of these, including forming, setting options and tips for success.

RINGS

Rings are a challenge because of the shrinkage issue. To make a wearable ring in a specific size, one must take the percentage of shrinkage into account. There are many different devices to ensure the finished size, including ceramic forms, permanent investment forms and single-use forms. Some devices are to prevent the ring from shrinking too much, while others just keep the round shape during firing.

Since Art Clay Silver's metal clay shrinks between 8 percent and 10 percent every time, you only need to remember to increase the size of the ring between 1.5 and 2 sizes, depending on the shape and thickness of the ring. See the Appendices for a reference chart that details pre-firing shape and size.

RING-MAKING TOOLS

Mandrels

A mandrel serves as a core around which metal, glass, wire or other materials can be cast, molded, forged or shaped. For metal clay, you'll want a wooden mandrel. Why wood and not metal? Two reasons: First, wood is lighter and can be handled when it's hot. Second, metal expands when it is heated, even with a hair dryer or dehydrator, and it may actually change the size of the ring.

Mandrel Holders

I've tried balancing mandrels on my lap or on a table, and neither is desirable. There are several mandrel holders available on the market. Choose one that fits your needs. The one I prefer has a hole in the large end of a tapered mandrel and fits onto a metal L-shaped stand. The mandrel can be rotated for decorating or shaping, and the stand can be positioned horizontally or vertically for drying.

Ring Sizers

Once you've selected your mandrel and mandrel holder, it's time to determine the ring size. There are metal and plastic ring sizers of all shapes. Two of the most popular are traditional ring sizers and adjustable plastic sizers. Whichever sizer you use, it's important that the sizer fit exactly as a ring would.

Preparing the Mandrel

1 Use a sizer to determine the size of clay ring you need to make. Use a pencil to mark the size on the wooden mandrel. I use either a reusable metal or plastic ring sizer and make two parallel marks on my mandrel.

2 Wrap a strip of thin, nonstick work surface around the mandrel over the marks; overlap the ends and add ¼" to the length before you trim the strip. Place a very small piece of clear tape lengthwise over the seam, and burnish it with a fingernail. It won't want to stick (it is, after all, a nonstick surface), so take the time to burnish it well so it won't come off. Because the mandrel is tapered, the nonstick strip will be slightly off-center when taped. This is normal. The strip must be snug and have no gaps between it and the mandrel.

3 Rotate the strip so you can see your pencil marks through it. Your mandrel is now ready for the clay.

Ring-Making Tips

Here are a few general tips to make great rings:

- Always cut on a diagonal — not straight across — to maximize the surface area that will be attached.

- Use syringe-type clay (not paste type) to attach the ends of the seam. Syringe type is thicker than paste type because it has less water, and it will hold the ends together better until the shank dries.

- When attaching the seam, insert syringe-type clay between the two ends, and ease them together. Don't put the ends together and add the syringe type on top.

- After adding syringe type, use water or paste to make sure the syringe type has joined the two ends together.

- Before you dry a ring, check the straightness of the shank. Whether your shank is coiled or flat, you will have a very difficult time correcting any waviness or angulation after you dry it.

- To straighten a ring shank before drying, use a straightedge, either a ruler or measuring slat, to check the shape as you rotate the mandrel. Don't use a craft knife or other sharp object, as you'll cut the shank rather than adjust it. If you see that the edge isn't straight, use the straightedge to gently push it back into shape without changing its size.

- After the ring has set on the mandrel for about 10 minutes, remove it so that the side against the nonstick surface can be exposed to the air. This is important, since the nonstick surface is impermeable. Even after long periods of drying, you may find that the inside of the ring remains moist after it is removed from the mandrel.

- If a ring doesn't slip off of the mandrel easily, wrap your entire hand around the ring and gently twist it to release it. If the ring and strip come off together, pinch the strip to remove it. Then, continue to dry the ring.

- Don't roll the clay for a ring band too thin. Until you've become very experienced creating rings, you'll probably find yourself taking some time filing and sanding to perfect your ring surface. Unless you take this into consideration, you may find yourself with a ring that is too thin and susceptible to breaking after firing.

- When adding clay or appliqué elements to a green ware ring, make sure you use plenty of paste type to attach them. Poorly attached elements will pop off during firing or polishing.

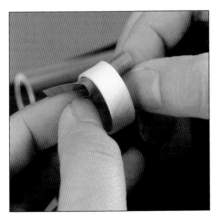

ROUND-SHANK RING

One of the biggest challenges in creating a round-shank ring is rolling an even coil to create it.

Using your fingers is the least-desired method, since it not only is impossible to roll a perfectly sized coil, but also, your fingers will draw precious moisture from the clay.

Rolled-Coil Shank

The best way to make a perfect coil is to roll something flat over the clay. You can use a piece of flat plastic or glass. There are products created for this express purpose. Even pressure is placed on the coil as it is rolled, and to elongate the coil, pressure is changed to the front or back while rolling.

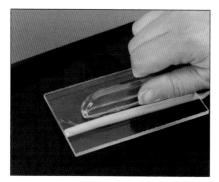

The coil must be free of folds and major cracks that go into or through the clay. Surface cracks can be filed away after drying, but internal folds or cracks will remain and weaken the piece.

The worst thing to do is add water or paste to the surface and cover cracks up. This only will hide the cracks; it won't solve the problem.

To connect the seams on a round shank, it is important to place the ends side-to-side when cutting off the excess. This prevents the ring from being too large.

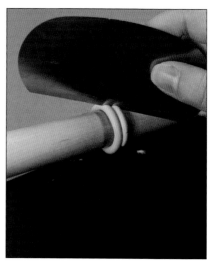

Wrap-Around Shank

A second round-shank ring technique is called a wrap-around shank. With this method, the coil is wrapped from the back to the front, and the ends are exposed on the top of the ring, either side by side, or on either side of a central, decorative element.

Since a poorly formed shank will be diagonal instead of straight, it will be longer, and, therefore, the ring will be too large after firing. After forming the shank on this type of ring, you must make sure the underside of the ring is straight, and snug up the ring if needed.

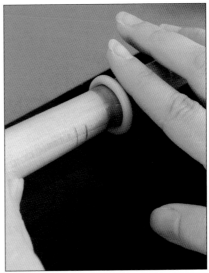

Either way, there are two challenges with this type of shank: to connect the ends adequately so the ring is a solid piece when fired and to make sure that the underside of the ring is straight.

FLAT-BAND RINGS

The main difference between flat-band and round-shank rings (other than the obvious) is that a flat-band ring can, by its width, change the actual size of the finished ring needed. This is because we all have a fleshy pad on our fingers, between the joints. Round shank rings, typically thinner, ride over that fleshy pad and settle in the crease between the pad and the palm (or joint).

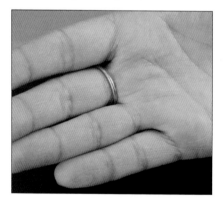

The flat-band ring, which is wider, may sit directly on the fleshy pad, so it needs extra length to fit the increased diameter.

Another difference is that the ends of a flat-band ring can't be placed side to side to cut them, because they're too wide. The ends must be placed on top of each other, cut diagonally (as are the ends for a round-shank ring), and then repositioned.

You need to ensure that no gap exists on the mandrel between the clay and the nonstick strip. If there is a gap, trim the ends of the band again and snug them together.

To make sure your ring is a consistent width, you can use a measuring mat or pre-lined graph paper as a guide when trimming your clay.

Of course, you can — and should — file and sand your ring evenly after drying, but these steps will save you a lot of time and effort.

Clay Type Vs. Paper Type For Shanks

I know of artists who use Paper Type to form flat-band shanks. In my experience, clay type is the superior choice, as it is safer and more advantageous than Paper Type.

I've already talked about the drawbacks of Paper Type in relation to its hydrophobia (not the frothing-at-the-mouth type, but the disintegration that can occur if water comes into contact with the fragile sheets). In my opinion, there are other concerns with using Paper Type for the main body of a ring.

Among the two choices of anhydrous metal clay, Paper Type is twice as thick as sheet type. That means that sheet type often is used as two layers that have been laminated together using a minimal amount of paste type for strength. That said, you may need to attach appliqués to the surface in order to provide more support, no matter what brand you use. These appliqués can be used to hide and reinforce the seam, because, as you know, putting syringe or paste type on the seams is potentially dangerous.

BRAIDED RING

A braided ring is sized exactly the same as any other ring. The difficulty most people have is in cutting the braid at the seam so the design is not totally compromised. Here's the best method I've found.

1 Overlap the ends on the mandrel and locate where one of the braid lines crosses diagonally. Put your cutting tool right beneath that braid line and cut diagonally, parallel to it.

2 Remove the excess clay.

3 Ease the two ends together after adding syringe-type clay.

4 Use paste type to smooth the seams of the separate ropes of the braids.

5 Dry well.

6 If the design is still mismatched, use syringe-type clay to recreate the detail.

7 After drying, use a round file to sculpt the braided design.

CARVING A DESIGN

Deciding to carve a design into the top of a ring requires the safety of added clay so that the carving doesn't weaken the ring by thinning or breaking through the surface.

Preparing a Ring for Carving

There are two ways to create a thickened ring top: add clay after the band is created or create a brand-new band where the clay is rolled so the middle is thickened before the clay is wrapped around the mandrel. The second method has the advantage of saving time, as the ring shape is created at the same time as the shank.

Adding Clay to an Existing Band

1 Roll out a small log, thinned at each end. Place it on the seam, which will reinforce the area.

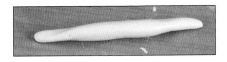

2 Smooth the thinned ends into each side of the shank. Make sure the clay is added evenly.

Thickening A New Band

1 Roll the entire shank of the ring, but leave the middle thickened.

2 Wrap the shank around the mandrel. Trim and connect the seam as usual.

3 Once the seam is joined, dry the ring with the seam down, since the extra clay's weight would separate the seam if it was on top.

SETTING STONES

As the art of metal clay progresses, we find more and more ways to use stones that can be fired directly in the clay. There are, generally, three groups of gemstones.

NO-FIRE STONES

The first group of gemstones is comprised of those that cannot be fired in place at all. The reason isn't always because they would be destroyed. Sometimes, as in the case of the topaz and quartz families, the stone would survive, but the color would be adversely affected.

In addition to topaz and quartz, this category of stones includes turquoise, agates, opals and organics, such as pearls and coral.

LOW-FIRE STONES

The second group is composed of stones that can be fired at low-fire clay temperatures (1,200 F to 1,300 F), but that wouldn't survive at standard clay temperatures.

There are a few stones — specifically garnets — that might be able to be fired at the higher temperature, but it's iffy. The garnet family comprises a host of names and colors, from traditional red to orange, mint green, bright green and many in between. I say it's better to play it safe and fire all garnets within the low-fire range.

In addition to garnet, this category of stones includes peridot, hematite and obsidian, among others.

HIGH-FIRE STONES

The third group of stones is the hardiest. These stones would survive any metal clay sintering temperature.

There aren't many in this category, but they're a great bunch: Corundum (rubies and sapphires, both synthetic and natural, though there's a caveat here); spinel; cubic zirconia (totally man-made); chrysoberyl; alexandrite (if you can afford it); and a few others.

The caveat I mentioned about man-made vs. natural high-fire stones is that natural stones nearly always have imperfections, called inclusions, that may include air bubbles, tiny fractures, bits of other material, etc. When heated, these inclusions may cause the stone to shatter, fracture or otherwise weaken.

Although very small, natural stones (1 mm to 3 mm) would probably fire without any problems — and I've used these sizes on many occasions — larger natural stones are expensive enough to generate a bit of nervousness at the thought of possible damage during firing. The final decision is yours, but the risk is real.

FIRING A STONE IN PLACE

In all instances of setting and firing stones in place, it is important to remember that, prior to firing, all vestiges of metal clay must be removed from each stone's surface. Any traces left behind will be permanently attached to the stones as silver specks or "fuming," which will appear as a silver haze over the surface of the stone.

Here are two methods to fire stones in place.

Insert the Stone Into the Clay

The first — and easiest — method is to directly insert a stone into the clay prior to firing.

To successfully capture the stone, the widest part of the stone (the girdle) must be below the clay surface. If the girdle is not captured by the clay, the stone will pop out of the hole when the clay shrinks.

Before the stone is set, some people prefer to use a straw that is smaller than the stone's diameter to make a hole so the stone is open on the reverse side, which has several advantages. It decreases the amount of displaced clay that can distort the piece as the stone is pushed in, and it allows the stone to be slightly suspended in the hole. It also allows the light to pass through the stone and be reflected back.

Coil Bezel

The second method to fire a stone in place is to use syringe-type clay to prepare a coil bezel of sorts. This method is handy when the piece is too thin and pushing the stone into the clay would force the point of the faceted stone (the culet) to hit the work surface beneath the piece.

Use the medium nozzle on the syringe to extrude syringe-type clay in one continuous spiral that circles the edge of the hole three times. This spiral must be slightly smaller than the diameter of the stone.

Set the stone onto the top of the coil, and gently press it down so that the syringe type pushes up over the girdle of the stone and locks it in place.

After drying and firing, the metal clay will capture the stone in a thin bezel.

READY-MADE SETTINGS

For faceted gemstones that cannot be fired in place, the only recourse is to set the stones after firing. That requires pronged settings that are able to withstand sintering temperatures.

Before there was low-fire metal clay, the only silver that could withstand firing with standard metal clay was fine silver. Consequently, pronged settings of various sizes and shapes were developed in fine silver. These pure silver settings were pushed into the clay, and the shrinkage during firing locked them in place.

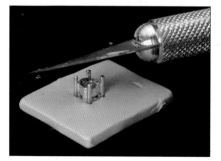

Since the introduction of low-fire metal clays, traditional sterling silver prong settings are an alternative. However, the firing temperature must remain below 1,300 F to avoid fire scale from occurring in the alloy.

After sintering, place the stone in the setting. Close the prongs over the girdle, beginning with opposite prongs. Finish by rocking the prongs fully against the stone.

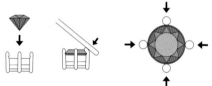

For cabochon-shaped stones, there are flat-bottomed, bezel-cup settings that can be fired in place so the stones can be placed in after firing. Paste type must be put around the settings to secure them during firing.

Custom Settings

There may be times when traditional settings are inappropriate, unavailable, or undesirable. Custom settings are uniquely different, and they vary from situation to situation.

Fine Silver Wire Prongs

Prongs made from fine silver wire offer one option when you want to include an unusual shaped stone that can't be fired in place and/or, which you can't or don't want to use a flat bezel wire.

1 Bend small pieces of round, fine silver in half and crimp them together.

2 Impress the stone into the clay initially to get a general size and shape. Then, set the raw ends of the bent wire into the clay outside of the impression to allow for the metal clay's shrinkage.

3 After firing and polishing, set the stone in place. Bend the wires, which now are prongs, around the stone to capture it.

Syringe-Type Prongs

There may be occasions where you want to use a stone that can be fired in place, but, because of its shape, depth or another consideration, it can't be set into the clay.

One way to set this stone is to create "prongs" by using syringe-type clay. These prongs are placed directly on the stone, however, this method cannot be used on stones that must be set after the metal clay is sintered.

1 Attach the "prongs" to the green ware of the base, and end them over the girdle of the stone.

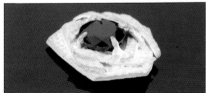

2 After drying, shape and file these prongs as desired to appear more natural.

Flat Bezel-Wire Setting

The most common method of setting cabochon-shaped stones that are of an unusual size or shape is to use flat bezel wire, which is pressed into the clay prior to drying.

Clay shrinkage during sintering locks the bezel in place. This bezel wire has been commonly made of fine silver, but sterling bezel wire can be used with low-fire metal clays. The flat wire comes in many widths and profiles; choose what you need depending on the stone's depth and desired look.

1 Shape the wire around the stone, and trim the ends very straight. The frame can't be so tight as to lift the stone with it when raised or so loose that you can see space between the stone and the bezel.

2 After the ends have been filed and the seam fits perfectly together, put a small amount of Oil Paste over the outside of the seam. Never put it on the inside, as it will hinder the proper fitting of the stone after firing.

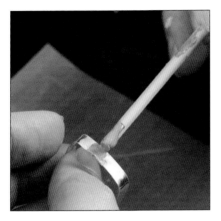

3 Dry the piece thoroughly. Fire it at 1,472 F for 30 minutes; torch firing is also appropriate. If necessary, file the piece slightly, but avoid filing it too much or the seam will break through again.

4 Create the base of your piece thicker than normal, as the bezel must be set into the clay at least ⅓₂". If the bezel is pushed into the clay too deeply, it will break through the bottom during firing.

5 Place paste type inside and outside of the perimeter of the bezel to fill in any gaps. Do not over-paste inside the bezel, or the stone won't fit properly after firing.

Flat Bezel-Wire Setting Tips

- Don't use wire that is too deep for the stone. This causes the wire to pleat or pucker when it closes around the stone. This is the biggest mistake made with this method.

- Choose the proper temper of bezel wire; softer is better. The harder the wire is, the more difficult it will be to bend it around the stone. You want "dead soft" wire, rather than "half hard." Dead soft wire will be very pliable and very easy to form around a cabochon.

- It is common for the bottom of the piece to become slightly concave, even if the bezel is set properly. This occurs because the clay shrinks around the bezel wire, but the wire itself does not shrink.

- After firing, place a punch or another small tool inside the empty bezel, and flatten the piece by tapping it slightly.

- Don't tap directly on the bezel wire, or you will damage it. If, on the other hand, the bezel is set too deeply, it may break through the bottom of the piece during firing and create an ugly crack (or cracks) that must be repaired before you go any further.

• The bezel should barely cover the part of the cabochon where the stone begins the slope to the top, also known as the shoulder. If the bezel wire is too tall, don't close it. Instead, cut a piece or pieces of plastic or nonstick work surface to raise the bottom of the stone. This will cause the stone to sit higher and the bezel wire to rest lower on the cabochon when it is closed.

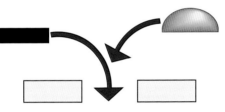

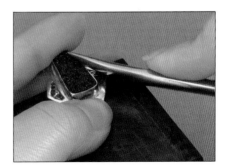

• Check that the stone is level in the setting when it is placed into the fired bezel wire. Adjust it as needed. Use a bezel pusher or agate burnisher to firmly but carefully roll the bezel wire against the stone. Repeat this several times around the stone until the bezel is closed and no gaps remain between the bezel and the stone.

FINDINGS

BROOCH FINDINGS

Two different types of brooch findings are made specifically for metal clay.

One has pieces that can be fired in place, and pieces that must be attached afterwards. The pieces that can be fired are made of fine silver; the remaining pieces are made of base metal or other metals that would weaken during firing.

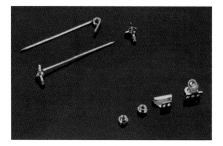

Three-Piece Setting

The three-piece setting consists of a safety catch and head, both of which can be fired, and the pin, which must be attached after firing.

1 Dry the piece.

2 After determining the distance needed to have the pin tip rest under the safety catch after firing, use syringe and paste type to set the two fine silver pieces in place.

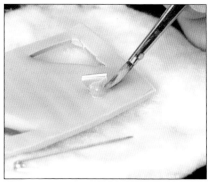

3 Use a pliers to clamp the pin between the two sides of the head.

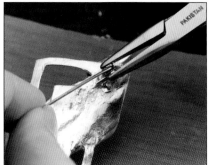

Four-Piece Setting

In this setting design, there are two tiny, threaded, fine silver bolts that are pressed into the clay.

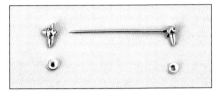

After firing, the safety catch and hinged pin are screwed into these bolts. While this brooch setting looks more professional and is longer lasting, it is definitely more difficult to set in place.

The biggest challenge with this system is that the pin catch and hinge, when screwed in, must face the correct direction. If the bolts are misaligned, the pin may face the wrong way from the safety catch. For that reason, it is suggested that the catch and pin be screwed in to the bolts prior to setting the bolts in place in the clay.

1 Dry the piece.

2 Gently unscrew the two upper pieces without moving the bolts. Continue with the procedure as outlined. Once you determine the distance needed to have the pin tip rest under the safety catch after firing, use syringe and paste type to set the pieces in place.

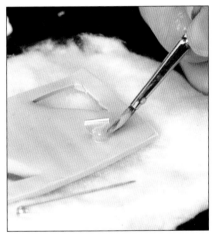

3 Use a pliers to clamp the pin between the two sides of the head.

Syringe-Type Spiral Setting

If your piece has dried but it is too thin to drill holes, you can create a setting by making a spiral with syringe type, much like creating a bezel setting for a stone as mentioned previously.

1 Place the bolts into the raised coils and paste them securely.

2 If you are going to set the bolts into wet clay, make sure that they are not pressed in so far that the tiny threads are contaminated with clay. If this occurs, the brooch parts won't screw in properly after firing.

3 Once the bolts are pressed into the clay, carefully set paste type around the bolts to secure them.

4 Dry the piece well, and fire it.

5 Carefully screw in the catch and hinged pin. Set a drop of glue on each where the threaded pins meet the bolts.

Hanging Findings

There are many prefabricated, fine silver findings available for use in metal clay.

Flat Screw Eyes

Flat screw eyes are a variation of the round screw eye, a larger version of which is still used in wood.

The tiny, flat screw eye isn't screwed in at all, but rather slid into the wet clay all the way to the round "eye" part, which opens front to back.

A dab of paste fills in any gaps between the clay and the finding. As with all findings, the clay will grab the screw eye during firing. A snap-on bail or other bail can then be attached to the screw eye for use with a chain.

Wire Loop

A wire loop can be used in lieu of a flat screw eye. It can be shaped like a horseshoe or a staple, but it needs at least two points of attachment to be strong enough. Attach with syringe and paste types.

Invisible Bail

The invisible bail back is a prefabricated piece of fine silver shaped much like a human ear.

It has two tabs that rest flat against the green ware. The tabs are adhered with syringe- and/or paste-type clay, and then are completely covered with paste type.

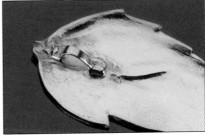

The bail itself rests unseen behind the piece, and only the chain is visible.

CHAPTER 7
MANIPULATING, MIXING AND MATCHING MATERIALS

Metal, metal and more metal. Fine silver, gold, brass, copper, even sterling silver: They all can be mixed and matched like a summer wardrobe, with metal clay being the "little black dress" that goes with everything!

MANIPULATING GREEN WARE

SCULPTING

Metal clay sculpting can be completed at any stage, wet or dry. For sculpting done at the wet stage, the tools tend to be smaller and more delicate than those used on large, sculpted works of earth-based clay, but the techniques are the same.

After the clay dries completely, sculpting is best done with a rotary power tool, which minimizes chipping and possible cracking. Personally, I love sculpting in this stage. All of the residue can be recycled back into paste, and I love using all the small diamond tips I have for metalworking.

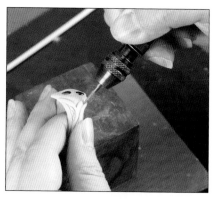

Remove, smooth, shape and cut away. You can achieve extraordinary detail by using Slow Dry formula, keeping your clay moist, working in small sections, drying the piece and then assembling it. Cookie cutters, clay cutters and other tools can help minimize the clay's exposure to air while you are sculpting.

Be warned, however, that using a rotary motor tool on dried metal clay isn't like working on finished metal. It cuts like butter, and an inattentive moment can turn into a quick disaster. Of course, with metal clay, anything can be repaired, replaced and returned to its original form, but with time as valuable as it is, the less you have to spend doing repairs, the better.

The best tip for sculpting is to use the right bit for the right job. Don't use a pointed bit to grind a round hole, and always, always, look more than you grind.

ENGRAVING

Drawing in wet clay, even superficially, makes a bit of a mess. All of the displaced clay dots the surface, and it has to be filed and sanded away after drying.

A better engraving method is to wait until the whole piece is dried, then use a file or a rotary power tool with a fine-tip attachment to carefully and methodically engrave your design.

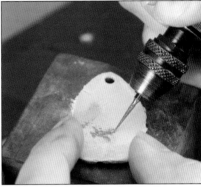

The excess clay, now a powder, will be removed much more evenly, and it can be recycled easily. The finished design will have a cleaner edge and take less time to prepare for firing.

TIPS FOR SUCCESS

+ If you are using straight files, choose the right shape for the design. If you are carving a design, you might do better to use a V-shaped or triangle file instead of a round file. After firing, the straight sides of a triangle file will be more reflective than the curved sides made by a round file.

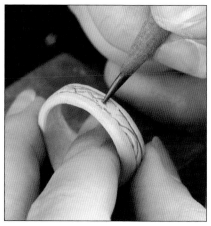

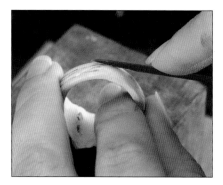

+ Use a pencil to draw your design onto the green ware. The graphite will burn away when the piece is fired, and the marks will keep you on track.

+ Keep your edges and depths even. Stay symmetrical.

+ Tap and brush your files often to keep the teeth clean. In the same respect, brush your piece often to keep the clay dust out of the design and make it easier to follow.

+ If you are using power tools, wear a mask or respirator to minimize your lungs' exposure to the dust.

REPAIRING GREEN WARE

CRACKS, PITS AND FOLDS

Folds, pits and cracks happen as a matter of course. If you see a fold in the wet clay as you're forming it, the best thing you can do is stop, add a drop of water, knead the clay, rework it and reform it.

A fold is a disaster waiting to happen. It won't repair itself once the piece is dried or fired. A fold is a gap that traps air. During firing, it actually will get larger, as the sides of the fold shrink away from the gap. After firing, the piece will be weak at that point and may break under normal wear.

If you see a fold in dry green ware, add a liberal amount of paste to the surface and wait a minute or so for the moisture to transfer through the fold. Smooth the surface to compress it, and the moister clay may fill in some of the inner space. Then, add syringe type to the surface to seal the opening and strengthen the surface.

The same goes for repairing cracks and pits. You can use paste, but syringe type is thicker and tackier and it is used more like spackle than paste.

The secret to success and time management is to overfill the defect. Think of it as repairing a crack in a plaster wall. If you smooth the spackle over the crack and let it dry, the spackle contracts, and you have to refill it. If you overfill the crack, it levels out when it dries, and you can just sand it smooth.

Breaks

Partial Breaks

If a break doesn't go all the way through the piece, make sure you separate it just slightly, and force some syringe type into the partial break.

Then add more syringe type to the surface, allow it to dry and file or sand it smooth.

Complete Breaks

If a break is complete, make sure you add syringe type to the inside of both edges before you put them together.

Let the excess squeeze out the sides, and smooth it with paste type. Add more syringe and/or paste type as needed, allow it to dry and file or sand it smooth.

Multiple Breaks

If you have multiple broken pieces, such as a ring that has fallen or (more often) been squeezed a bit too hard, put the pieces together first, like a puzzle, to see what fits where. Then, start at one end and join two of the pieces.

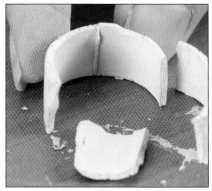

Allow it to dry, add another piece with syringe type, dry it again, and continue until the entire piece is together again.

Seams

We've addressed seams before. There's really no excuse for a seam to show, and a visible seam is also a point of weakness.

Take the time to join your seams properly, overfill them, dry them and sand or file them smooth. This little extra effort will make your piece stronger after the final firing.

Using Other Materials

Brass

Brass is an alloy of copper and zinc. Its melting temperature is 1,600 F, but it anneals (becomes softer and more workable) at approximately 1,000 F. Because of these properties, brass can be used with silver metal clay in a variety of ways.

The main thing to remember when firing brass with silver clay is that no molecular exchange takes place. The brass and silver don't combine in any way; the brass is held in place by the silver itself.

There are dozens of different types of brass, all with varying percentages of copper and zinc, and some may contain small amounts of one or more other elements, such as lead, tin, iron, antimony and phosphorus.

Brass Wire and Tubing

Small-gauge brass wire and tubing can be imbedded into metal clay. However, fire scale can appear when the copper in the brass oxidizes. To reduce the appearance of fire scale when firing at temperatures over 1,300 F, completely cover the brass with metal clay during firing, and keep the temperature of the brass at 1,480 F or less.

After firing, use files and sandpaper or a rotary power tool to expose the brass. Take care when removing the silver, as it can easily pull away from the brass. To avoid this problem, file in the direction of the brass wire (when at all possible), and use long, hard strokes.

If a space develops between the brass wire and the silver and gets larger with continuous filing, fill the gap with Oil Paste and fire the piece at 1,472 F for 30 minutes to repair it. Continue to file until the brass wire is exposed evenly. Use wet sandpapers or a rotary tool to create a mirror finish. If desired, a patina, such as liver of sulfur, can be used on the silver to darken it and increase the contrast between it and the brass, which will polish to a high, golden luster.

Fine Mesh

Another form of brass, fine mesh, can be combined with metal clay in different ways.

You can extrude clay through the mesh to create a checkerboard of tiny squares that can be shaped and fired as a decorative element.

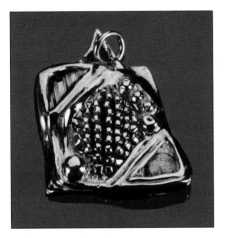

Fire the brass right in place, and trim any exposed pieces afterward.

With the advent of low-fire clays, brass also can be used as a vehicle to attach other design elements, such as beading.

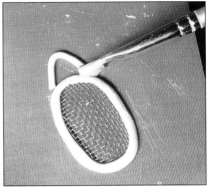

A wearable framework of metal clay can encompass a piece of brass mesh and, after firing, beads can be threaded and worked through the mesh.

Copper

Copper is one of the most important elements we have. This metal is used to form alloys, such as brass, bronze and sterling silver, and it has a melting point of 1,980 F. Although copper is resistant to corrosion, it will discolor at higher temperatures. When it is heated to or beyond annealing temperatures (1,000 F), copper begins to bond with oxygen to create reddish-toned cuprous oxide and then black cupric oxide.

At annealing temperatures, the fire scale is negligible, and the surface darkening can easily be buffed away. However, at temperatures above approximately 1,400 F, the copper oxidizes more, which blackens it significantly and weakens the copper structure.

Certainly combining copper with standard metal clay at firing temperatures of 1,472 F and above is problematic. But low-fire clays will combine with copper and its alloys (most importantly, sterling silver) with little or no negative affects.

Sterling Silver

The most important aspect of firing fine silver with sterling silver is to keep the sintering temperature below 1,300 F. This assures that the fire scale is so minimal, it won't compromise the metal's integrity. Like other metals, sterling won't bond to fine silver during firing.

Sterling silver must be captured in some way, usually by being buried in the clay, or secured with paste and/or syringe type. Any darkening of the sterling that does occur can be brushed or buffed away.

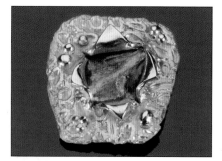

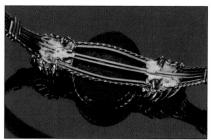

GOLD

CLAYS

Gold clays were developed at the same time as silver clays, but they always have been costlier. They are available in 22-karat and 24-karat varieties, and one variety is documented as firing at 1,290 F for 90 minutes.

Art Clay's 22-karat gold clay fires at 1,813 F for 60 minutes, which requires a kiln. The market price of gold in recent years has caused the use of solid gold metal clay to be fairly prohibitive, and it has resulted in inventive, alternative methods to add gold accents to silver and other materials.

If you use gold clay alone, use separate brushes and metal or plastic tools that are free of seams or cracks that can harbor expensive bits of clay. Wood is not, in my opinion, a good material for tools, as the grain usually is porous and will absorb gold-laden moisture.

I also feel that 22-karat gold is preferable to 24-karat gold, not only because the gold content is less and therefore, less expensive, but because pure 24-karat gold is generally considered too soft for everyday wear for jewelry.

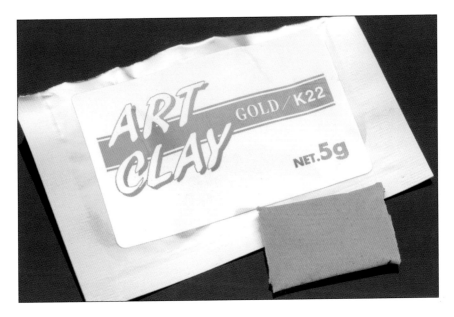

Gold clay can be mixed with water to make a mustard-looking paste.

Add this paste to green ware in three fine layers.

Torch firing is the best method to fire gold metal clay, during which the thin layer of gold sinters with the

silver. Some of the silver and gold ions exchange, and, after burnishing — preferably done while the piece still is hot — this layer will adhere permanently to the silver surface.

PRE-PREPARED PASTE

There are several brands of gold paste available on the market. They are either 22-karat or 24-karat gold and are comprised of gold particles suspended in some kind of binder. Most pastes are formulated only to be applied to and fired on silver. They can be applied to the piece and fired with a torch, a hot plate or a kiln.

Each brand has its own particular directions, which can be found in the packages and online. One brand of gold paste, however, is formulated to bond directly to other surfaces, such as ceramic and glass. Of course, it can be fired onto sintered fine silver as well, but the ability to fire to nonsilver items vastly increases its versatility.

Art Clay Gold Paste is 22-karat gold, mixed with a nontoxic, organic binder and water. It can be applied directly to fired silver and sintered in a kiln or fired with a torch. It also can be applied directly to glass and ceramic pieces like other high-fire art paints.

After it is fired in a kiln (other methods are not recommended due to the fragility of the glass, etc.), Art Clay Gold Paste is permanently bonded, and it can be burnished. If more intense gold color is desired, it is better to apply it in layers, and fire the piece after adding each layer.

FOIL

Gold foil is, typically, 24-karat gold in content, and it can be applied to fired silver in a Korean technique known as keum boo or keum bu.

This technique requires the foil to be attached to a heated silver piece and burnished while it is still hot. What happens during that process is that atoms of silver and gold exchange, bonding permanently through diffusion.

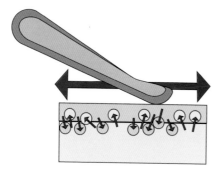

If it is heated long enough, the gold will lighten and then seemingly disappear, as the gold actually diffuses completely into the silver. This can be an advantage, however, in that layers of gold foil can be applied, one over the other, to give varying intensities of gold color to your piece.

Use a gold foil product suited for keum boo. Enameling foil and gold leaf are much too thin, and they will disappear into the silver before the process can be completed.

Either a hot plate or a kiln can be used for the keum boo technique, but a kiln is more precise and doesn't depend on visual cues.

Any burnisher also can be used, but I strongly suggest using an agate burnisher for several reasons:

+ Agate is strong, and it won't be scratched as easily as a metal burnisher would.

+ It doesn't conduct heat, as does metal, so it won't draw heat from the piece to the burnisher.

+ Agate won't stick to the gold foil when it is heated. If this happens to a metal burnisher, you have to cool the burnisher and quench it. Warning: Agate burnishers will crack if they are quenched in water while they are hot.

Keum Boo Technique

1 Meticulously clean the piece you are embellishing. This can be done with alcohol or by heat cleaning, which involves heating the piece to 1,000 F. This will destroy most dirt and oils on the surface of the silver.

2 Cut the piece of gold foil to the desired shape, and place it on the piece. The foil doesn't need to be just on edge or in a recess. Use a small, diluted drop of white glue to keep the piece of foil on your piece while moving it to and in the kiln, because convection currents caused by the heated air will move it.

3 Ramp the kiln to 1,472 F. Place the prepared piece on a small, cut section of fiber board. Open the kiln with one hand, and use a heat-resistant glove and tong to quickly transfer the fiber board into the kiln.

4 Close the door, and wait until the kiln again reads 1,472 F. Time a 2-minute period. At the end of 2 minutes, use a glove and tongs to remove the fiber board and silver piece, and set them on a heat-proof surface. Immediately stabilize the fired piece with the flat end of a long pair of tweezers. Use the shoulder edge of an agate burnisher to burnish all the surfaces of the gold foil onto the piece. Be sure to cover all areas of the foil.

5 If, for some reason, the piece begins to cool and you have not completed the burnishing process, you can return the piece to the kiln, allow the temperature to return to 1,472 F, and repeat the process. When you are finished, allow the piece to cool to room temperature.

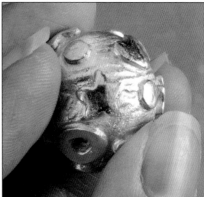

Combining Gold and Silver Successfully

There may be occasions when a solid piece of gold that has been fired first must be incorporated into a silver piece.

As with all other metals, solid gold and silver won't permanently attach to each other. Rather, the silver must capture the gold, such as in this gold and silver pendant. Therefore, fire the gold first, then imbed it into the silver clay. Dry and fire the silver as appropriate, then polish it.

CHAPTER 8
SILVER AND ...

Metal clay's extraordinary versatility in combining with other media — including glass, enamels, beads and polymer clay — makes it an artist's dream. No matter what your passion, metal clay can help you take it to new heights!

GLASS

Bits of volcanic glass and other glass formed in ancient forges were used as body decorations long before the art of glass making developed. The unusual properties of this silica-based art form amazed scientists for generations.

Volumes have been written about the properties and characteristics of glass, and we certainly can't address all of them in this book. But I will go over a few pertinent details as they relate to using glass with metal clay.

Glass has no real melting temperature. When heated, glass will transform from a rigid, brittle substance to one that softens enough to slump with gravity, lose its defined shape and eventually liquefy to a honey-like texture.

Upon cooling, as glass regains its rigidity, it goes through a stress-releasing period called "annealing." During the annealing process, any stress introduced to the glass, such as a change in temperature or incompatibility, is transferred to the glass, which will cause breaks and/or cracks.

Glass is a poor conductor of heat, whereas silver is an excellent conductor of heat. If you combine metal clay and glass and heat them together, then begin to cool them, the metal will cool a great deal faster than the glass will. If the glass has softened and is attached to the metal, the metal will try to conduct heat

from the glass faster than the glass will allow it, and the glass will crack.

The hotter that you heat the metal clay and glass, the more they will attach, the slower you must cool the piece in order for the glass to release its heat without breaking.

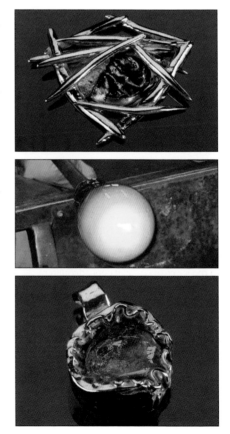

TIPS FOR SUCCESS

When you use heat above the approximate slumping temperature of glass (1,300 F), make an opening in the back of the metal clay piece prior to firing to expose the back of the glass. This will increase the surface area of the glass and allow it to release heat faster during cooling.

lose heat immediately and put a dangerous strain on the glass. Even though the temperature in the kiln might be low enough to be past the danger zone for annealing, an introduction of room air might cause thermal shock and breakage.

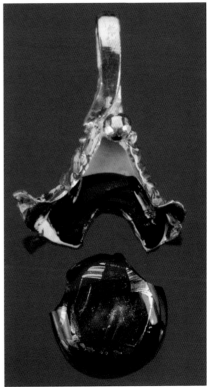

At temperatures below 1,300 F the glass generally won't soften enough to attach to the silver, and it will cool adequately without any additional openings.

Whenever glass is fired with metal clay, allow the fired piece to return to room temperature before you open the kiln. Any introduction of room-temperature air will cause the metal to

ENAMELS

BASICS

Enameling is the art of fusing finely ground glass onto metal. For our purposes, that metal is fine silver. The heat must be high enough to melt the glass, but low enough to avoid scorching it or melting the silver below.

Traditionally, enameling has been done on sterling silver and copper. Both of these metals oxidize upon firing and subsequently need to be cleaned in a pickling solution, also known as an acid bath, to remove the black coating, or fire scale, that results.

Fine silver, on the other hand, contains no copper, so it doesn't oxidize or create fire scale. Enamels can be laid down and fired without consequences to the silver other than the need to polish it. Typically, enamels on fine silver are fired between 1,400 F and 1,500 F.

There are many, fine books on enameling techniques, but as of this writing, there is only one with information specifically about enameling on metal clay. "Enameling on Metal Clay" by Pam East provides a wealth of information specifically regarding this technique.

SPECIAL TOOLS

Enameling in the kiln takes a few special tools.

A metal grate is the surface on which the piece for enameling rests. In order to transfer the piece to the kiln, raise the grate by bending each side.

An enameling fork is used to lift the grate and place it into the kiln.

Small sifters that have 80 openings per inch, called 80 mesh, hold the enameling powders and transfer them to the surface of the metal.

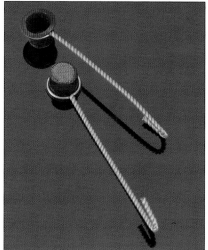

Distilled water is used to wash the enamels after fine sifting and remove any cloudiness. This step is more appropriate for "wet packing" enamels during champleve or cloisonne techniques and for transparent enamels.

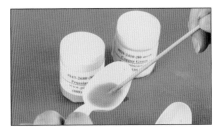

When you are simply sifting over textures, such as in basse taille, washing isn't essential.

A fine, 200-mesh screen is used to sift 80-mesh enamels prior to washing and wet packing. This will remove the cloudy, finer particles, which then are kept as counter-enamels.

A quarter or another coin of some weight should be placed in the screen while sifting, to avoid the fine powders flying into the air.

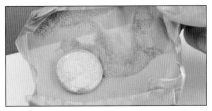

An alundum stone will level the metal and glass surface after the basic firings are completed. A final, flash firing at 1,500 F for a minute or so will have to be done after leveling to bring the enamel surface to a high gloss. The metal surface can be burnished or sanded to the desired finish.

A fiberglass brush is needed to clean the metal surface prior to enameling, and clean the enameling surface prior to relayering.

TIPS FOR ENAMELING SUCCESS

+ Use cool colors, such as blues and greens. They work better on metal clay than warm colors, which may overfire and change to unwanted colors.

+ Make the metal clay piece that is to be enameled slightly thicker than one you wouldn't enamel. If your pieces are thin, the enameling process may cause the metal to warp, which will crack the enamels. To prevent warping and cracking on a thin piece of metal, fire counter-enamels onto the backside to equalize the stress. Counter-enamels typically are made from a neutral color left over from remnants of other colors, and they are on the unseen side of the piece.

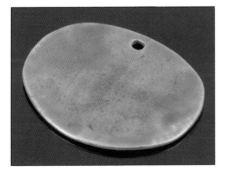

+ Avoid using syringe-type clay to create cloisons, or cells into which you put your enamels. The walls of the cells should be straight and perpendicular to the bottom surface. Using syringe type will result in a rounded side wall of varying thicknesses. When the piece cools, this structure will cause the enamels to be stressed, and cracks may result. An alternative is to use the syringe, then add thick paste where the syringe line touches the under surface. This will fill in the undercut area and solve the issue.

+ When you fuse multiple layers of enamels, it isn't necessary to reach the full-fuse, high-gloss firing stage every time. Prior to the glossy stage, the surface will resemble an orange peel. The piece can be removed at this stage. Only the final layer of enamel needs to achieve the high-gloss firing stage.

POLYMER CLAY

Polymer clay is moldable polymer plastic that comes in several brands and types, as well as many colors and transparencies.

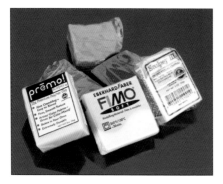

Polymer clays can be baked in toaster ovens, kitchen ovens or craft ovens; follow the manufacturer's directions. Because polymer clay is a type of plastic, overbaking can release toxic fumes, so always follow the baking instructions for the clay you use.

Any number of techniques are possible when you combine metal clay and polymer clay, including impressing a simple stamp, backing a cut-out design and attaching a metal clay accent as part of a finished, polymer clay project.

Including Polymer Clay

Metal clay always is fired first when polymer clay is added as a design element. Just as occurs when you combine metals with silver clay, polymer clay won't fuse or melt to the fine silver. An intaglio, or stamped design, must be present, or some other way must exist to attach the two types of clay.

Tips for Polymer Clay Success

+ Don't polish the surface of metal clay to be included with polymer clay. It will stick much better if it is slightly rough.

+ If you are using a stamp, make the impression deep and even, which will ensure that the polymer clay won't pull out after baking.

+ When you choose a polymer clay, read the information regarding flexibility, color change and durability. Also, if you are looking for a finished shine, check to see which brand will give you the look you desire.

CERAMICS

Ceramics refer to inorganic, nonmetal materials that usually include clay or other earth minerals. They are crystalline compounds. The kind of ceramics used in art forms with metal clay are silica based.

When mixed with water, ceramics can be formed, shaped, sculpted and sanded. When fired at temperatures higher than the melting point of silver, they become rigid and vitreous. Clear or colored glazes can be added, and the piece can be refired to give it either a low gloss or a high gloss.

Unfired but dry clay objects are called green ware. Pieces that have been initially fired but remain unglazed are called bisque or bisque ware. Often, kiln firing of ceramics is done using temperatures based on varying sizes of ceramic cones, which, on some kilns, control when a kiln shuts off by sagging at a particular temperature. Hence, firing at a particular "cone" means firing to a particular temperature.

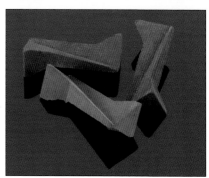

BISQUE WARE

One of the unique ways to use metal clay is in the art of doll making. For hundreds of years, the heads, hands and sometimes feet of children's dolls were hand-carved and fired bisque ware. Today, master doll makers still practice this craft and spend hundreds of hours creating the faces, bodies and costumes for dolls of all shapes, sizes and designs.

Since the heads, necks and extremities are bisque ware, there is no difficulty firing metal clay onto these surfaces. Necklaces, rings, bracelets and even clothing can be attached to the bisque surfaces and fired before the doll is assembled.

FAUX RAKU

Another method to enhance ceramics is to apply paste type to the entire surface of a bisque piece. Usually, a minimum of three layers is needed; pay close attention to edges and engraved details. After firing, burnish the entire surface by hand or with a rotary tool.

Apply liver of sulfur patina in as brilliant of colors as possible. When done correctly, the surface of the bisque ware will imitate the complex and difficult reduction firing ceramic technique of raku.

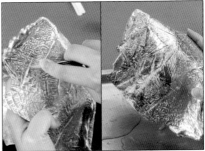

Patricia Walton

STENCILING

Before the advent of the low-fire metal clays, attempting to attach metal clay to glazed ceramics was iffy, at best. Often, the fired silver would pop or peel off. Low-fire metal clay pastes fare somewhat better, but only Art Clay's Silver Overlay Paste is formulated specifically to bond to nonporous surfaces. It has a unique binder that is tackier than other silver pastes. It can be stenciled, brushed and painted on fired, glazed ceramic. Burnishing and polishing after refiring brings out the high, silver shine.

It's easy to stencil a glazed ceramic piece with Overlay Paste.

1 Clean the surface of the piece with alcohol. When it's dry, attach the stencil to the surface and press with a flat object to get all of the edges attached.

2 Use a cosmetic sponge to apply undiluted Overlay Paste to the piece. Dab over the stencil until an even layer is applied. You can use a paintbrush, but dabbing produces the best results.

3 Let the Overlay Paste dry completely. If you don't, you're likely to smear the design when you try to remove the stencil.

4 Peel the edge of the stencil, and lift it straight off.

5 Use a toothpick to clean up any edges of the stencil.

6 Fire the piece at 1,200 F for 30 minutes, and allow it to cool.

SGRAFFITO

Sgraffito is a technique by which a thin, diluted layer of Overlay Paste is floated over the surface of glass or ceramic, a design is transferred to the Overlay Paste by carbon paper or other means, and the background is scratched away while the design remains.

Adding a sgraffito design is the very last thing you should do before firing. The layer is so fragile that if any mois-ture gets on the design or it's disturbed in any way, you'll have to fix it.

1 Clean the surface of the glass or ceramic meticulously; use alcohol, if possible.

2 Dilute the Overlay Paste with drops of water to thin it to the consistency of skim milk. The goal is to make the Overlay Paste nearly translucent. If the layer is too thick, it will chip off when you attempt to scratch it off.

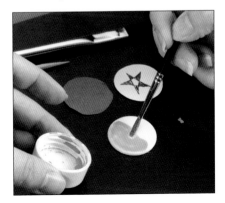

3 Add the Overlay Paste to the piece.

4 Lightly trace the desired design through the carbon paper. You don't want to press so hard that you actually scratch into the Overlay Paste layer.

5 Use a sgraffito tool, a thin bamboo skewer or a polished metal point to scratch away the Overlay Paste. Avoid using something so sharp that it damages the glazed surface. Keep the picture of the finished design nearby so you can refer to it. It's very easy to get confused and scratch away part of the design which should have remained, while leaving parts that should have been scratched away.

6 After you've scratched the background away, brush gently, but thoroughly. Use a brush, like a disposable flux brush, to brush away the Overlay Paste that you scratch off.

7 Use a toothpick dipped in alcohol to remove any remaining specks of Overlay Paste. Anything left on the surface will be fired permanently to the ceramic.

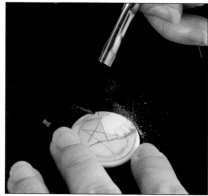

8 Fire the piece.

9 Polish the fired sgraffito design. Use an agate burnisher first, followed by metal polish.

Beads

What is easier than rolling a ball of metal clay, piercing it with a toothpick and firing it? Not much, if you ask the increasing number of beading artists who have begun using metal clay to embellish their creations. Whether you create the focal bead of your dreams, spacers between gemstone beads or a framework (as was previously mentioned) around wildly beaded brass mesh, metal clay makes the unique even more so.

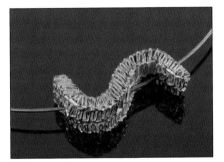

There are so many ways to create beads with metal clay that the mind boggles. Choose a shape. Choose a texture. Add color, a patina or let the silver shine. There are more books written about metal clay with, and as, beads than any other kind.

Openwork Beads

Openwork beads are one of my favorite kinds of beads. They are created by extruding syringe-type clay over a cork clay form.

1 Make a cork form. Push a bamboo skewer through as a mandrel.

2 Allow the cork to dry totally, so when you squeeze it, there's no give at all. This is important, because you don't want any moisture left in the cork, because it will turn into steam during firing and damage your bead.

3 Use your syringe to lay down lines in any way you like. I like the net effect; to achieve it, apply overlapping rows in alternating layers.

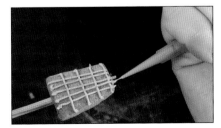

4 Ensure the lines go right up to the skewer without touching it with your syringe. If you do, an ugly spot may be left behind when the skewer burns away.

5 Place a small dot of paste type everywhere the lines overlap. Remember that the cork is going to burn away; all of the overlapping rows must touch and be connected as a whole piece. If not, the bead will fall apart during firing. Remember: Metal clay will shrink away from a gap, so the lines will pull apart unless they're connected well.

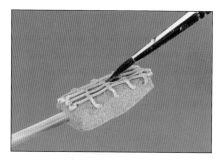

6 After the bead dries, examine it. Use 600-grit sandpaper to smooth any sharp points.

7 Prop the bead carefully on fiber blanket, and fire it to 1,300 F for 30 minutes. This should give the cork time to burn out fully.

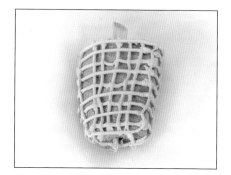

8 When the bead is cool, rinse out the cork ash, and place the bead in a rotary tumbler. Fill the chamber with 2 pounds of stainless steel, mixed-shape shot, two-thirds of a chamber of water, a splash of jewelry cleaner and a squirt of dish liquid. Let the piece rotate for at least 90 minutes before you check it. If shot gets caught inside the bead, shake gently until it is removed.

9 Rinse the bead well, and dry it. Now, isn't that the coolest thing you've seen?

Tips for Bead Success

+ I know I've said this before, but don't, don't, don't fire Styrofoam or any other plastic! It isn't worth the risk, and the environment will thank you!

+ When you dry a metal clay bead on a mandrel, you don't have to hold it until it dries! Cut notches on opposite sides of a paper or plastic cup, and suspend the mandrel and bead between them.

+ If the bead is on the end of a wooden skewer or toothpick, stick the skewer into a small block of unfired polymer clay.

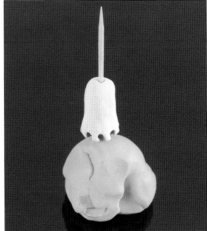

RESINS

SELF-CURING RESINS

There are three main types of self-curing-curing resins used in the craft/hobby/art industry: epoxy resins, polyester resins and two-part urethane resins.

Epoxy

Epoxy resins use two equal parts of a long-chain polymer resin and a catalyst. The curing time is fairly long: usually overnight, but you can speed it up with a hair dryer. The clear epoxy resin has enough time to cure so that any air bubbles trapped in it have time to rise to the surface and pop. However, it is difficult to sand and polish if the surface gets marred during curing. Colorants and other additives are available to create imitations of gemstones, glass, etc.

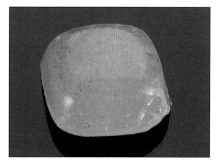

Polyester

Polyester resins have a separate hardener that is added by drop to the actual resin. Curing occurs fairly quickly, and the results are quite brittle.

Safety and health risks are associated with polyester resin; be sure to read all of the instructions and follow the manufacturer's recommendations. Polyester resins also have very strong, noxious odors; mix them outside or in a space that has adequate ventilation.

Urethane

Urethane resins are two-part, short-chain polymer resins that come in clear formulas. The clear formula is ultraviolet stable, which means it won't discolor in light. Dyes are available as colorants.

One of the main advantages of urethane resin over epoxy is its ability to be manipulated in a very short time. It has a quick set-up time, around 5 minutes, and it can be removed from any mold in 30 to 45 minutes. You can create many more designs, and the surfaces can be wet sanded and polished without difficulty.

However, this quick cure time also is a disadvantage, since minute air bubbles don't have time to reach the surface and break before hardening. Vacuum degassing is suggested, but that takes special equipment, which isn't available to most of us.

Urethane Resin Tips

+ To minimize air bubble formation in clear urethane resin, don't whip the contents when you mix the two parts; rather, fold them together.

+ When you pour urethane resins into a mold or piece, pour slowly and from a short distance. Pour the resin into one side and tap as you pour.

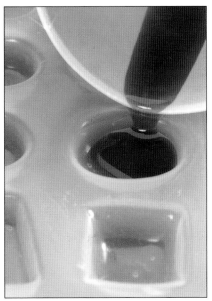

- If you don't want to pour resin into a mold, you can make a metal clay frame and pour the resin directly into the void, perhaps over dried flowers or a glossy picture.

- To imitate gemstones like amber and opal, mix clear urethane resin with colorants and certain inclusions.

- To imitate enamels, pour urethane resin over foil or a textured metal clay base.

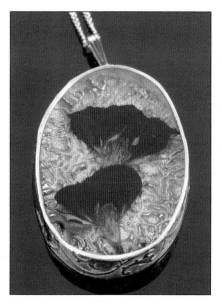

Ultraviolet-Cured Resins

As the name implies, ultraviolet-cured resins need a separate UV light source to cure.

These resins cure very quickly, in approximately 30 seconds. Layering and color gradations can result in extraordinary effects. One of the biggest advantages is that the resin will stay viscous until you're ready to cure it. There's no time crunch, and small bubbles can be avoided by simply heating the resin in a toaster oven or warm stove. With the discovery of cost-effective UV lights — those used in the nail industry are perfect — and colorants, there's no end to the possibilities. Of all of the resins used with metal clay, UV resins are, in my opinion, the easiest to use and most versatile.

Low-Fire Enamels

Low-fire enamels aren't enamels at all, in the traditional sense of the word. They are specially formulated, water-based paints that are either transparent or opaque, and they can be baked to permanence in a regular kitchen oven.

Because of this ease of use, low-fire enamels are perfect to add color to metal clay in the absence of a kiln or the desire to use traditional enamels.

My low-fire enamel choice for metal clay is another one of Pébéo's lines, Vitrea 160.

Created originally for use on glass, I've found that Vitrea 160's wonderful transparency is perfect for metal clay.

The paints are water soluble, and they can be mixed like those on a painter's palette. They are also self-leveling, which means that you won't leave brush strokes during application.

Pébéo, a company in France that produces extraordinary art colors, has created a line of low-fire enamels for use on a wide range of surfaces. The Porcelaine 150 line, which fires at 150 C, was created for ceramics. Pébéo has opaque, transparent and metallic colors, and the colors are as vibrant and stable after firing as before. The piece must dry for 24 hours prior to baking.

After allowing the piece to dry for 24 hours, bake in an oven at 325 F for 40 minutes.

Low-Fire Enamel Tips For Success

+ Never put the paint on metal clay green ware. Metal clay must be fired first.

+ Make sure the surface has been cleaned with alcohol before you apply these paints.

+ When you open the bottle, stir the paint with a toothpick.

+ Use a soft brush to apply low-fire enamels.

+ If a spot of paint lands where it doesn't belong, wait until it dries. Then, use a toothpick to rub off the unwanted spot.

+ Don't rush the drying: 24 hours means just that. If you don't wait at least that long, you may find that the paint has tiny bubbles in it after firing.

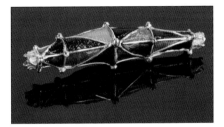

+ If you live in a moist environment, you can place the painted piece in a warm toaster oven during the drying phase.

+ Do not put your piece on a metal plate in the oven. If necessary, put the piece on glass, and place in the oven before you turn it on.

COLORED PENCILS

The ones that work best are those that are waxy, such as the Brand name Prismacolor. They come in dozens of colors and can be placed right on the silver. However, the colors are best applied over an acrylic pre-coating called "gesso." Gesso is typically used by artists to prepare canvas, and comes in clear, white, black and grey. By applying a thin layer of white gesso first and allowing it to dry, the pencil colors will adhere evenly. In addition, having them on white makes the colors appear brighter and more identifiable. I've found that the slightly grainy consistency of the colors after application can be smoothed by using an agate burnisher.

As with all colored pencil applications, the surface must be protected by a clear coating so the colors won't come off. You can use a spray lacquer, polyurethane coating or, my favorite, clear UV resin. This will make the colors even brighter.

Use colored pencils to draw small backgrounds or centerpieces for your metal clay. It's another inexpensive way to apply color and make your pieces even more original.

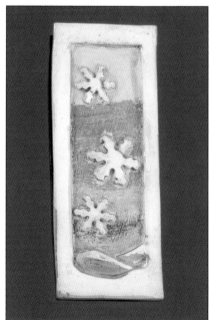

Fine Silver and Sterling Silver

Prior to the appearance of low-fire metal clays, firing sterling silver at the standard sintering temperature was prohibitive, as it caused weakening and fire scale.

Firing at 1,200 F however, allows for the inclusion of all kinds of sterling: findings, bracelet blanks, wire, even ring blanks.

For findings, it's important to remember that the sterling won't actually stick to the fine silver on firing; it must be captured or incorporated into the design with syringe or paste type.

I've successfully included sterling silver ear posts with a flat base into metal clay earrings. Because you don't want the sterling post spinning in the metal clay, however, use a small file to rough up the lower post and base to give it "tooth" and prevent it from turning after firing.

The same goes for pronged settings. It's not enough to press the setting into the metal clay. You need to bury the bottom in paste or syringe type prior to firing. This way, when the metal clay shrinks, it will lock onto the finding.

Speaking of shrinkage, this is the most important consideration when firing large pieces of sterling, like bracelet blanks, with metal clay. When you attach metal clay to large areas, the metal clay is likely to crack on shrinking.

If and when this happens, apply Overlay Paste or Oil Paste to the areas, and refire the piece.

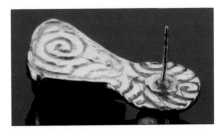

Jane Levy

Jane Levy

If you want to add a solid, decorative element to sterling, lay down a layer of Overlay Paste first, as an intermediary. Then, attach the solid metal clay piece to the Overlay Paste, and allow it to dry.

Chapter 9
Tips and Troubleshooting

There is always "just another thing" that someone forgets to tell you when you're learning something, usually after you've done that "thing" wrong. Here are a few other things that I think are important to know. I hope that I've told you in plenty of time!

Troubleshooting also is an essential part of knowing any medium. It's easy to tell when things go right; it's much harder to figure out why things go wrong. I've included some troubles we can shoot together.

Firing

Firing Temperatures

For some reason, people find it very difficult to remember what to fire, when and for how long. And nice firing charts (one of which is included in the Appendices of this book), only seem to make matters worse.

Most metal clays have a sliding scale of firing: If you fire this at this temperature, then you fire for this time. If you fire at that temperature, you fire for that amount of time. It gets very confusing. When you add another element, like glass or ceramic, the entire scale changes!

And, just in case you think you're getting it straightened out, the different brands are different enough to make it impossible to settle on just one temperature. There are all kinds of in-between temperatures, "what-if" temperatures, and "It's Tuesday, so we have to fire it higher" temperatures out there. At least, that's how it appears.

If you're looking at a way to remember the low-fire, high-fire, when, where and what to do in the kiln, try my simplified approach. I remember 1,300 F, 1,472 F and 1,600 F: period. The times may change a little, but for all intents and purposes, I only have to remember those three temperatures, and that's less chance to get confused.

1,300 F

+ **1,300 F for 30 minutes.** For all general low-fire firing conditions, 1,300 F for 30 minutes will get the job done. It's a little more than the lowest temperature (for those of you who like to fire as high as possible for that added strength they tell you about), but it's not so high that it will hurt glass or sterling that you've added to your piece.

1,472 F

+ **1,472 F for 5 minutes.** This is the turning point for the low-fire clays. After this temperature and all the way to the highest firing temperature of 1,600 F to 1,650 F, you only need a 5-minute firing.

- **1,472 F for 30 minutes.** If you still fire standard clays (those that typically fire to 1,600 F to 1,650 F for 10 minutes), Oil Paste and Paper Type, this is the temperature and time for you. Don't confuse it with the previous low-fire temperature.

1,600 F

- **1,600 F for 5 minutes.** This is the high-temperature limit for most metal clays. No, a 50-degree swing up to 1,650 F won't matter. But if you're firing low-fire clays, you need at least 5 minutes here.

- **1,600 F for 10 minutes.** This is the minimum time and maximum temperature for standard metal clays (give or take that 50 degrees we talked about). Remember that the melting point of silver is 1,761 F, so you don't even want to go near that!

Supporting Dimensional Objects in the Kiln

There have been entire chapters on, and scores of e-mails written about, the use of certain propping methods for dimensional pieces in the kiln. Obviously, you need to make your own decisions. But, I'll share my experiences and impressions, if they help.

Alumina Hydrate

This very fine, powdery substance is used in glazes and kiln wash.

I advise against using it as a pile in the kiln, where the hot air currents will cause it to become airborne. It's not because I believe it's toxic, but because it's so fine that it's easily inhaled, and it is not good for your lungs. With all of the other options out there, it's unnecessary to use such a fine powder in the open.

Vermiculite

This mineral is heated to expand it into a lightweight, granular material. It's fire resistant, absorbent and used as an insulator and additive in gardening.

The vermiculite available for purchase in North America now is safe and effective. Some time ago, certain vermiculite was found to have been contaminated with asbestos, but that has been removed from the market.

That said, like alumina hydrate, vermiculite can be dispersed into the air by the heated, convection currents inside and outside your kiln. Take precautions when working with loose materials. If you have asthma or are sensitive, wear a mask or respirator.

Fiber Blanket

This compressed, ceramic fiber is used extensively in the hot glass industry.

Fiber blanket is heat resistant, and it can be molded and reused many times. Small pieces can be ripped off to place in the crevices of intricate pieces. Fiber blanket can be used both to prop up and hold down.

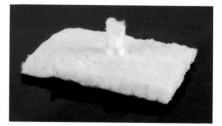

The fibers are larger, so are less irritating to the lungs, but you still might want to wear a mask. My advice: Go with the largest fibers possible. Our lungs don't like anything but air.

TORCH FIRING

Torch firing is a very acceptable alternative to kiln firing. That said, you must pay strict attention to the color of the metal while using the torch.

Metal color is absolutely, positively the most important factor for success — not distance, not time. Sintering is achieved by the peachy, salmon color of the hot metal. If you let it get too red, you'll reach the melting point, and the silver will melt. If it does not reach the color that indicates sintering, the pockets of air that were created by the burning off of the binder will remain, and the piece will still be brittle after firing.

Tips for Torch-Firing Success

♦ Use an approved fire brick as a surface. Using a ceramic brick can be dangerous, as heating one spot to high temperatures may cause the ceramic to crack or splinter.

♦ Trace an outline of your piece prior to firing. If you don't see a perceptible difference after firing, there wasn't enough shrinkage, which means that sintering wasn't accomplished. Refire.

- Make sure you're timing from the proper glow of the metal, and not from the time you turn on the torch.

- If you're having trouble seeing the glow of the metal, dim or turn off the lights in your work area.

- Make sure your piece is absolutely dry before you begin torch firing, especially if you're using a Slow Dry formula. Remember those "Alien" babies?

- There are size and volume restrictions. Don't try to cheat. If you try to fire a piece larger than a silver dollar or more than 25 grams of clay, you'll be disappointed. The metal clay manufacturers have given us these parameters for a reason. If you make the piece too large, you won't be able to keep the entire piece at the same sintering temperature at the same time. If you give the piece too much volume, the outside will sinter and the inside won't be able to keep up. Distortion, underfiring and even cracking may result.

- You can fire gemstones with a torch, but, in my experience, only those under 5 mm in size. If they're larger than that, I fear that cooling may cause them to crack. Never quench any piece with gemstones in it.

Why Torch Fire?

- Well, if you don't have a kiln or a gas stove, there's not much other choice. I think the torch is superior to the Hot Pot and about the same as the Speedfire Cone System.

- If you only have one piece to fire, it's fast and cheaper than firing up the entire kiln.

- It's not any more dangerous than any other method of firing. All methods need strict attention to safety, and no method should be left on and unattended.

Stove-Top Firing

With this method, seeing that salmon/peach glow of the metal is even more important to success.

Most of us don't know the exact Btu our stove puts out, so we depend on visual cues to tell us when we've reached the proper sintering temperature. If you don't see a glow, even after you've placed the piece to be fired on one of the areas that looked cherry red, stop the cycle. Without a visible glow, sintering will not occur.

It's also very important to leave the piece on the stainless steel net for a full

20 minutes after the 5-minute firing cycle is complete. This is a vital part of the sintering cycle; removing the piece earlier may cause it to remain brittle and be susceptible to breakage.

PRE-FINISHING

As my mother always said, "You can't make a silk purse out of a sow's ear," (although I suspect there's somebody out there who's tried). Actually, it wasn't my mother, but I agree with the sentiment.

If you don't do your polishing work prior to firing, you'll have a heck of a lot harder time achieving a mirror finish afterward, at least not the mirror finish I'm thinking of.

Let's go ahead and define "mirror finish." It's a finish that, after polishing, resembles a mirror. That means you can either see your reflection, or that of someone holding the camera to take a picture.

Shiny but cracked and bumpy is **not** a mirror finish. Neither is kind of smooth and shiny, or really smooth but kind of shiny. Don't think that throwing every piece in the tumbler is going to give you a mirror finish, either, unless you've spent some time in the green ware state with sandpapers or the like.

Silver is an incredibly shiny metal, and we in the relatively new medium of metal clay tend to forget that. Just because we can patina something doesn't mean that we should!

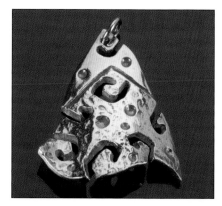

Sandpaper comes in all forms and shapes, mounted on rubber, wood and paper. Please use it! 400-grit, 600-grit and 1,200-grit sandpapers all are needed prior to firing to achieve a mirror finish.

So why sand now, rather than later? Mainly and most importantly, because it's easier! Second, when I sand and file prior to firing, I can gather up all those little, littler and littlest pieces of dried clay and recycle them.

going to lose 8 percent to 10 percent (or more) of the volume in shrinkage. If you use your agate burnisher before firing, it will be all shiny and make you feel good, but you're for sure going to lose that into thin air when the binders burn off.

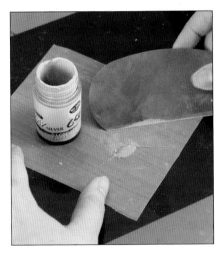

I'm not a metalsmith, and I don't want to refine finished silver. I want to use every, single bit in the clay state.

Some people swear they should sand with 2,000-grit paper prior to firing, or use a metal or agate burnisher. Personally, I think it's a waste of time. You're

Save your effort and, instead, use a damp cosmetic cloth or moist hand wipe to wipe off the surface of your finished piece prior to putting it in the kiln.

It will remove all vestiges of clay dust, and give your surface that look so important to achieving that "baby-butt" smooth finish.

POLISHING

HAND POLISHING

Is there really a difference? Can you tell the difference between a hand finish and a rotary-tool finish? I hope not. Art Clay World USA teaches fine finishing by hand. Why?

First, because not everyone has a rotary power tool. Second, because we can. Choosing not to finely finish a silver piece is not the same as not knowing how to finely finish a silver piece.

Third, there's nothing like the feeling of looking at yourself reflected in a piece of your jewelry and knowing that you achieved that by yourself.

To me, that's an important part of the artistic process. Do I use a rotary power tool? Of course I do, especially when the design is complex and I can't do, physically, what the tool can do. But, honestly, there are times when I've polished something with the power tool and been dissatisfied with it and gone back and done it over by hand with wet sandpapers. It's probably all in my head, but then again, maybe not...

MIRROR FINISH BY HAND

1 Give the piece a good brushing; use a stainless steel or brass brush.

2 Clear your work surface of everything but a cup of clean water, your sandpaper of choice and your rubber block.

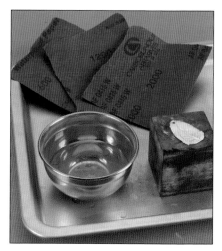

3 Fold a small piece of 600-grit sandpaper in half; you don't want to use a piece larger than a couple of inches square.

4 Wet the sandpaper in the clean water, wet the piece, and wet the paper again. Prepare to get wet — sloppy wet. You must rinse the piece and the paper frequently, or this will take much, much longer than it needs to.

5 Begin by sanding in one direction; you'll only sand in one direction with the 600 grit. Put some muscle into it. Get into a comfortable position, with the work surface not too high, or you won't be able to get any leverage behind it. Rinse the piece and paper every 30 seconds or so.

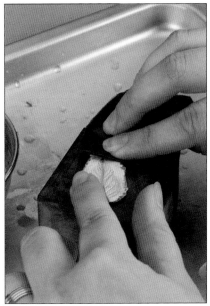

6 If you have scratches or imperfections that won't come out with the 600-grit sandpaper, stop sanding! Switch instead to the smallest file that you have. After all, polishing is really just creating finer and finer scratches in the surface of the metal. File in one direction — away from you — and work in strokes to remove the scratches.

7 Check the piece after every stroke, and stop filing immediately once you observe that the scratch or imperfection is gone. Then, go back to the 600-grit sandpaper and start over.

8 Once you get an even surface (it should take about 5-7 minutes), clean off your block, rinse your piece and change the water and sandpaper. This step is vital. If you don't get rid of the 600 grit from your work surface, you might drag it onto your piece during the next step, which will put scratches right back on your piece.

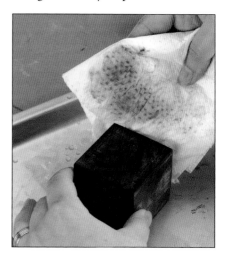

9 With clean water, block, piece and a fresh piece of 1,200-grit sandpaper, begin to sand perpendicular to the direction you used when sanding with the 600-grit sandpaper. Rinse both the piece and the sandpaper often, and use your weight to work evenly over the surface.

If you've sanded properly with the 600-grit sandpaper, it shouldn't take more than 5 minutes' sanding with 1,200 grit.

10 When you finish sanding with the 1,200-grit sandpaper, wipe the block, change the water and switch to a very fine sandpaper, such as 2,000 grit. Wet sand with the 2,000-grit sandpaper for another 5 minutes. At this point, it should be very even and very shiny, it won't be that mirror finish yet.

11 Decide if you want to sand with 4,000-grit sandpaper. I think it's unnecessary, especially if you've done everything right to this point and you use Wenol after sanding. I think that sometimes you see scratches after using 4,000-grit sandpaper that you didn't see there at 2,000 grit.

12 Rinse the piece well, and dry everything, including the block.

Machine Polishing

For those of you who want to try machine polishing, there are dozens of brands of tips, wheels, bands and shapes of polishing tools. Again, it's a matter of using successively finer and finer abrasives to create a good finish.

Most machine polishers don't use water, so friction will generate a certain amount of heat in your metal piece when you get to the higher grits.

The unfortunate part about purchasing ready-made abrasives is that they rarely are marked with the actual grit. Most have vague notations, like coarse, medium, fine, extra fine, etc. That's really meaningless. Is coarse 120 grit or 240 grit? Is extra-fine 2,000 grit or just 1,200 grit? That's why I like to know what I'm using.

I have my own particular silicone polishing discs that are color-coded to let me know what comes next. I take my time, and, for the most part, I'm happy. I

get cylinders that screw onto a threaded mandrel, and I can carve them to a point if I need to. When my pieces are very dimensional and complex, I really can't argue with the rotary tool that spins at 20,000 revolutions per minute.

The very last thing I do, no matter which method of polishing I use, is explained next.

WENOL: THE JEWELER'S BEST-KEPT SECRET

I'm a lapidary. I learned how to cut and polish stones and opals, and I've been doing so for many years. I've used red rouge, Tripoli polish, all kinds of things, and I hate them all. They're nasty, they get all over, and it takes forever to get it all off your piece after you're done.

Then I found metal clay, and after that, I found "It."

What is "It"? It's the most wonderful, most incredible, most underappreciated metal polish on the planet. And, before you ask, no, I don't own stock in, have a vested interest in or get kickbacks from the company. "It" is Wenol, a metal polish from Germany, though we don't get it directly from there.

You know how that very famous cook, with his own show and orchestra, says "Bam!" when he adds that special ingredient? Well, for me, Wenol is metal clay's "Bam!"

Wenol takes that fine finish and kicks it up a notch — into the stratosphere. Ask anyone who's used it. Bam! You can pull out my fingernails, but I'll never give up my Wenol.

When Art Clay World, USA, senior instructors-to-be send in their three pieces for jurying and I look at their mirror-finished piece, I can tell right away if they were told about Wenol. If not, I grab my cloth and start polishing.

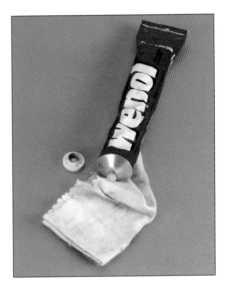

Using Wenol

1 Squeeze less than ⅛" of Wenol out of the tube and onto a soft, nap-free, lint-free cloth, like an old T-shirt.

2 Work the Wenol into the cloth for a second, and then give your piece a good rub with the same pressure you used with sandpaper.

3 Rub the piece all over until the treated area on the cloth is nice and black. Then, use a clean area of the cloth to buff what you just polished. I'm willing to bet your eyes will widen appreciably. Welcome to the world of the mirror finish!

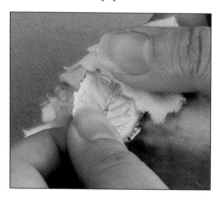

HAND BURNISHING

Sometimes, you're pressed for time, you have a little spot you want to shine, or you've added a thin layer of overlay or gold paste and you don't want to get too aggressive. These are the situations where you might choose to hand burnish your piece.

To burnish a piece, hold the burnishing tool close to its head, pressing down on the surface of the metal and rubbing the burnisher back and forth with pressure on the piece.

Burnishing compresses the surface of the silver in order to decrease porosity and increase shine. You'll immediately see the shine as the metal is compressed. It won't demonstrably change the surface texture, however, so if you have cracks and imperfections, they will remain.

The two most common tools used to hand burnish are the metal burnisher and the agate burnisher.

Metal Burnisher

The metal burnisher may be straight or curved, thin or thick. The burnishing end is highly polished to reduce the chance you'll scratch the metal surface.

Agate Burnisher

The agate burnisher typically consists of a bamboo handle that has been bonded to a polished agate head. Agate burnishers usually are knife-shaped, but there are other shapes as well.

Hand Burnishing Tips

+ Burnish in small circles, and be sure to overlap your strokes. Avoid long strokes, which will be more visible.

+ When you've completed the entire area to be burnished, finish with a polishing cloth and Wenol.

POWER FINISHERS

Typically called mass finishers, these machines use some kind of medium that will repeatedly hit the piece and perform the same basic function as the hand burnisher.

Rotary Tumbler

The rotary tumbler is my personal favorite power finisher.

This form of finishing serves a number of purposes. First, it shines. Second, it provides some degree of work hardening on the metal. This means that as the media pummel the piece and hit it repeatedly, they cause the surface of the metal to become less porous and stronger to a much deeper extent than hand burnishing. In addition, where hand burnishing may take minutes, the rotary tumbler performs this polishing for at least 90 minutes for fine silver, during which time I can do other work. Third, the rotary tumbler polishes those items that may be too fragile to hand burnish, such as filigree or openwork metal clay items.

So, how is throwing 2 pounds of stainless steel shot on your piece for more than an hour gentler than hand burnishing? My guess is because there is less pressure and more time to achieve similar results. All I know is that it works.

> **TIP**: Get a heavy-duty motor for the 3-quart capacity tumbler, because stainless steel shot is heavy, and the cheap models just aren't meant to drag all that weight around and around and around.

The Contenti Company

Magnetic Tumbler

The magnetic tumbler uses pin shot (small, straight pieces of steel) that sit at the bottom of the chamber and are spun against the piece.

According to most manufacturers, magnetic tumblers work best on intricate pieces with deep grooves and detail — not flat pieces. Personally, I don't think magnetic tumblers do as good of a job as rotary tumblers, but, again, that is my personal preference.

Vibratory Finisher

The vibratory finisher does not tumble the media; it shakes it, along with your piece.

Some people prefer it; they claim it takes less time. Personally, I don't see the difference, and there are some stones that I would rotate that I wouldn't shake. It's a personal preference.

Ultrasonic Cleaner

The Contenti Company

This is the one method that I never use. First, ultrasonic cleaners really are meant for cleaning, not shining. Second, I often use stones that might not survive the ultrasonic waves. So, just to play it safe, I stick to my trusty rotating tumbler.

Patinas

Liver of Sulfur

Yes, it stinks. There: We've admitted it. But darn, it really works, too.

Just as there are dozens of recipes for making bread, there are dozens of recipes for mixing just the right batch of liver of sulfur, also known as sulfurated potash. Every one of us claims that our recipe is the very best way to get all those gorgeous colors.

Well, I can't give you all of those recipes; you'll just have to try as many different ways of mixing liver of sulfur as you can, and choose the one you like the best. For what it's worth, however, I will give you mine.

Liver of Sulfur Recipe

- 1 cup steaming — not boiling — water
- 1 thumbnail-sized piece of liver of sulfur
- 1 cup of cold water for rinsing
- Silver wire to dunk the piece
- 1 capful of plain ammonia (optional)

Liver of Sulfur Basics

No matter what recipe you use, there are some absolute certainties with liver of sulfur.

- If you don't absolutely clean your piece, you won't get a good result. How do I clean my pieces? I use a paste of baking soda and water, rinse thoroughly, and pat dry. Then I don't touch my piece again.

+ The more polished the piece is before patinating, the better the colors will be. Don't believe me? Check out an unbrushed piece straight from the kiln, a brushed but matte piece, and then a polished piece. Dunk each piece for the same amount of time in the same-temperature solution. You'll see what I mean.

+ Liver of sulfur will cause fine silver to turn the following colors in the following order: gold, amber, magenta, blue and black. If you're lucky, and have some variation in additives — some people swear by potassium salts — you might get some greens thrown in with the blues.

- Controlling the color is part luck, part timing, part heat and part preparation. Those are a lot of parts, but it isn't an exact science.

Some artists swear that if you heat the piece, it works better. Others say it will work better if you have a weak solution. I think that keeping it hot and dipping quickly in the solution, then quickly into the rinse water to stop the reaction is just as good of a way as any. I do know that if you take your sweet time when you dunk, by the time you get to your rinse water, you'll have shot past your desired color. In my opinion, if the solution gets too cool, it will take much longer, and those intense colors you're looking for may be more difficult to achieve.

- Don't look at your piece after dunking but before rinsing. As you watch, the colors will continue to change. Rinse the piece to stop the patinating process, then look.

How to Maintain Patinas

Once you have those perfect colors, how do you keep them? We've been looking for the miracle solution for some time. Here are some tried and not-so-true methods:

- **Beeswax or renaissance wax:** In effect, you're coating the surface of the piece and protecting it from the sun and air. Effective but puts a film on the piece that you can feel.

- **Spray polyurethane coating:** This works, but it changes the colors and dulls them.

- **Glossy coating for low-fire enamels:** Again, this coating changes the colors.

- **Gloss protectant for auto paint:** This is a promising method. The colors are, for the most part, unchanged.

- **Plastic bag:** Storing a piece in a plastic bag doesn't add anything to the piece, and it protects it from air. Remove the piece to wear it or display it, and return it to the bag when you are done.

- **Spray lacquer:** This compound has an amber tinge to start with, and it alters the colors.

Let's face it. Anything you put on the surface that alters the light waves going through it will alter the colors. My solution is to store the piece in protective plastic bag or use nothing at all. I can always dip it again.

SILVER BLACK

I know people use silver black, but not me! I'd rather take stinky liver of sulfur any day. Silver black is also known as muriatic acid solution, which is yet another name for hydrochloric acid.

Thankfully, the solution is diluted, but it will wreak havoc with you, your lungs and any other metal surfaces it gets on. Plus, it has only one color: black. There are too few positives for me to use it, but, as always, the choice is yours. Just read all of the safety literature on either of these products before you decide which one you want to use.

PATINA DO'S AND DON'TS

+ Do use dry liver of sulfur and not premixed liquid. The premixed liquid has a limited shelf life and weakens when exposed to light. If you don't use it often, it will lose strength. However, the dry liver of sulfur can be made up fresh every time.

+ Do mix up a fresh batch of liver of sulfur liquid every time you need it.

+ Do dispose of the liver of sulfur liquid as soon as you're finished with it. Run cold water down the sink and flush the solution, then follow it with more water. It won't harm your pipes.

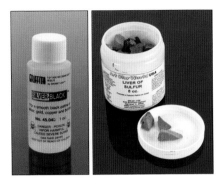

+ Don't worry if you leave your piece in too long or you don't like the color you got. You can remove the liver of sulfur by using a torch for 20 to 30 seconds until the piece turns white again, or you can put it in a kiln to 1,000 F and remove it. Polish the piece again, and redip it to get the desired result.

+ Do try different recipes. You might come up with something completely different!

+ Do work in a well-ventilated area and keep your jewelry and other pieces you don't want patinated away from your work area.

+ Don't put freshly patinated pieces in your tumbler! The liver of sulfur will come off on your shot, and everything you tumble after that will become patinated!

MASKING PATINAS

What do you do if there are parts of your piece you don't want to patina?

There are several ways to apply a "mask," which is a fancy way of saying you want to put some kind of barrier on some parts of your piece. This way, when you dip the piece or brush on the patina, it won't stick to those places that have the mask.

Permanent marker can be used to draw a design on parts of a fired piece.

After dipping the piece in the patina, use acetone or nail-polish remover to dissolve the marker and reveal the original silver.

Rubber cement will work, but it's difficult to control in small spaces, and it needs to be rubbed off fairly vigorously, which may mar the patinated parts of your piece as you remove it.

Masquepen is a latex-based solution made to apply with small and very small applicator tips. Draw any design, and allow the blue-tinged fluid to dry.

Dip the piece into the patina, and the places under the Masquepen will not darken. After you're done, just rub the piece or rinse it under water, and the resist comes right off.

Stencils and resist paper, both of which have a sticky side, can be used to protect areas of your design from the patina solution. Firmly attach stencils or resist paper to the piece to prevent the darkening solution from flowing under them.

MAKING REPAIRS AND CHANGES AFTER FIRING

OIL PASTE AND OVERLAY PASTE

Both of these products achieve the same goal when used to repair or add to fired silver.

Oil Paste is oil based, so it needs to be thinned and cleaned with the solvent that comes with it, or any mineral spirits. It must be fired at 1,472 F for 30 minutes, so it isn't intended for any pieces that must be fired at lower temperatures, such as pieces that include glass or certain gemstones.

Silver Overlay Paste is water soluble. It should be fired to at least 1,200 F for 30 minutes. It should be used at full strength, and it works well to fill cracks and pits.

If you are repairing a full break after firing, and you can use Oil Paste because nothing prevents you from firing at 1,472 F for 30 minutes, you should do so. Oil Paste was created specifically for this purpose, and if it's used properly, it will do the job with no problems.

Your pieces must be clean and dry. You don't need to polish the areas of the break prior to applying Oil Paste. The white inside is normal; it is the appearance of the unaligned silver particles, not evidence of an underfired piece!

Repairing Cracks and Filling Pits

As with green ware, you don't want to cover up the cracks or pits in fired pieces, but fill them. Use a bamboo skewer to stir the repair paste, and roll it into the defect. Force the paste inside to fill up the defect.

Remember to overfill the repair site. After firing, file and sand the surface so it is even.

Sealing Bezel Wire Seams

The seam must meet as perfectly as possible. Fill just the outside of the seam with either Oil Paste or Silver Overlay Paste, then dry and fire it. You'll be able to file and sand the outside seam slightly before using the bezel.

Adding Findings

If you have a piece whose finding has fallen out, use either Oil Paste or Silver Overlay Paste to fix the problem.

Dip the finding in the paste, and reinsert it in the piece. Use a toothpick to reinforce the gap, then dry and fire the piece as appropriate.

If you've forgotten a finding totally (gee, that never happens!) do as you would if the piece were green ware. You'll need to use a rotary power tool or a hefty file to cut a channel for a missing flat screw eye, but you don't want to just plop it on top, you want to inlay it.

Overfill over the inset screw eye, and then dry, fire, file and sand the piece flat.

Making Connections

Basic Soldering

I haven't soldered in all of the time I've used metal clay. Well, I soldered during my stained glass days, but that was totally different. Let's say that I haven't had to solder anything to my metal clay or my metal clay to anything, or metal clay to metal clay since 2000, when I first became involved with the medium. I haven't had to, which is one terrific reason not to solder.

That isn't to say that I couldn't solder if I wanted to. But, because I don't have a metalsmithing background, I don't look for a reason to solder. I am quite content to miss out on something that can really be a pain in the butt.

Don't let anyone tell you soldering is easy. It may be easy once you learn it and have some experience, but that's something we've all heard about sometime or another. Soldering is about silver, flux, heat conduction, torches and solder.

It's unnecessary for me to go into all of the different kinds of soldering that are available; there are many excellent books on the subject. But it never hurts to know some terminology and basic steps.

Let's say that you fired a metal clay piece and realized that you forgot to make it thick enough for your bezel wire. And, shoot! You even forgot to push the bezel wire into the darned clay!

Aside from chalking this up to a bad day, an option is to solder the bezel wire onto your piece. (You also could use Oil Paste to attach it to the surface of your piece, but that would eliminate the need for this exercise, wouldn't it?)

Soldering Materials

- A torch of some kind.

- A tripod stand with a steel mesh on top, or a soldering brick.

- Flux of some kind. Liquid is preferred, rather than paste. Flux is a cleaning agent that permits the solder to flow and prevents fire scale from interfering with the process.

- Solder of some kind. The situation you're in will determine whether you need hard, medium, easy or extra easy. Personally, I always choose easy, whenever possible. For this particular exercise, cut up some small chips, or pallions, of solder.

- Pickle. This is an acid solution into which you put your pieces after soldering. It removes any fire scale that has formed during the soldering process. I use a flux/pickle combination, so pickle is unnecessary.

- Water and baking soda solution. When you're done, be sure to thoroughly rinse your piece to neutralize any remaining acids.

- Tweezers.

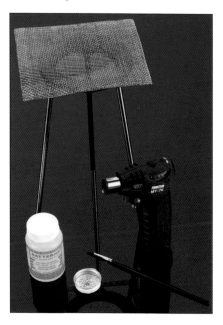

- Flux brush. I've read you shouldn't use a cheap brush, but unless you solder often, I don't expect this is vital.

Soldering Instructions

1 Clean the fired piece very well, as well as your bezel.

2 Flux the main piece generously.

3 Use the tweezers to place the bezel into position. It's very important that the bezel sit absolutely flat on the base, as soldering won't fill a gap!

4 Pick up a really small pallion and place it next to the joint on the inside of the bezel, which will prevent any excess solder from being seen on the silver.

5 Insert small pallions all the way around the inside of the bezel.

6 Heat the piece from the outside. Remember: Solder flows toward the heat. If you try to heat the solder, it won't work. Heat the piece until the flux bubbles as the water burns

away, leaving the flux behind; if you use an alcohol-based flux, this won't happen. If your pallions have moved, use the brush to move them back into position. Heat the fired piece well away from the bezel, from the bottom if it's on a tripod.

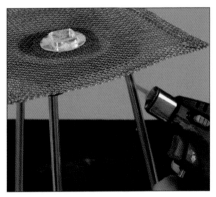

7 As soon as you see the solder begin to change, move the torch to the outside of the bezel, and heat it all around. When the solder flows, it will flow toward the heat, under the seam toward the outside. Stop heating immediately, and allow the piece to cool.

8 Pickle or rinse the cooled piece as needed. If we were working with sterling silver, we'd have nasty fire scale and we would have to pickle the piece. Since we're working with metal clay and fine silver, which have no copper, we just have to wash it in soap and water and we're good to go!

Tips For Soldering Success

Whether you're soldering a hinge, brooch findings or anything else, remember these tips for success:

+ Clean your pieces.

+ Flux well.

+ Use the right solder for the right situation.

+ If you have more than one soldering job, use the highest-melting solder first, so when you go to your second soldering, the first won't remelt!

+ Remember that solder flows towards the heat, so heat your piece, not the solder.

+ Use the least amount of solder you need.

COLD CONNECTIONS

Making cold connections means connecting things without soldering, melting or sintering. The two most common cold connections are eyelets and rivets.

Rivets

Rivets connect two or more pieces by means of holes through which a solid wire is placed. This wire is pounded flat on the top and the bottom, which prevents the wire from escaping. The rivet can be stationary, or it can be looser to allow movement between the parts.

Making a Rivet Attachment

This is one of several techniques to make rivet attachments.

Rivet Materials

+ 1" wire, 18 gauge
+ Wire cutter
+ Ball-peen hammer
+ Flat or center punch
+ Small vise
+ Hand or rotary drill and assorted drill bits

Rivet Instructions

1 Choose a drill bit that is the same size as the wire, and drill a hole in each piece. Make sure that the wire passes through without any gap. If the hole is larger, the spread head of the rivet won't prevent the wire from falling through.

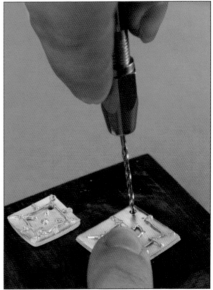

2 Put the wire into the vise so about ½2" shows. Place the punch on the end of the exposed wire, and use the hammer to tap the punch slightly around the edges to spread the wire.

3 Use the ball end of the ball-peen hammer to spread the head flat against the vise. Remove the wire from the vise, and thread the two pieces of metal clay over it.

4 Measure ½2" from the top of the metal clay piece (or half of the diameter of the wire or tube), and trim the wire.

5 Repeat the process of spreading the head of the wire; finish with the ball-peen hammer.

6 File the piece, and sand it slightly.

Eyelets

Eyelets are similar to rivets, but they are hollow tubes rather than solid wires. This allows a chain or other object to be threaded through the hole to connect all of the pieces. These connections are used instead of nails or screws where you want a permanent attachment with a flat profile on both sides.

Making an Eyelet Attachment

To make an eyelet, the steps are the same as those for a rivet, except that instead of using a punch to spread the head of the eyelet, use a hammer with a flatter end, like a jeweler's, or cross-peen, hammer.

1 Begin to spread the head of the eyelet; turn the hammer to avoid splitting the flange.

2 Switch to the rounded end of the hammer, and spread the eyelet flat.

3 Thread the metal clay pieces.

4 Repeat the procedure as needed.

METAL CLAY TROUBLESHOOTING

Here are answers to some common problems related to metal clay work.

CLAY PROBLEMS

Q Every time I roll a coil, fine cracks show up all over the surface. What should I do?

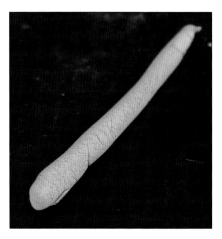

A The cracks are often unavoidable, but they are superficial. After drying, you should be able to file them away. Another solution is to use Art Clay's Slow Dry formula, which will give you more working time.

Q I find it very difficult to roll out my clay in a flat piece. It always seems to have bumps and ridges. How do I fix this?

A Even using cards or slats, sometimes it's difficult to roll flat. Try turning the piece 90 degrees every time you roll. That will even out the piece to a large extent.

Q Speaking of rolling, I use nonstick work surface, but after rolling, the clay is stuck so hard that I can't move it at all. What do I do?

A The object of rolling isn't to drive the clay into the work surface. Rolling should be a gentle motion, and you should turn the piece every time. If you do roll so vigorously that the clay won't move, let it dry in place for a minute or so. It should release enough to get it off of the work surface.

Q When I make rings, I can't seem to get the seams together right. They keep separating, and I make a mess. What should I do?

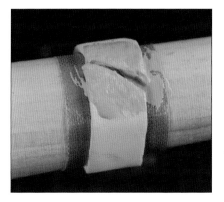

A Initial ring seams are the toughest. Make sure you're using syringe type to combine the two ends, not just paste type. Use the back of the paintbrush to smooth the seam and two sides together. Hold it for a minute to make sure the seam won't separate, and let it dry. You can add more paste and/or syringe type later.

Q When I use syringe type, my lines are flat and squished. How can I fix this?

A I love to use syringe type, but it's not the easiest technique to master. The important thing is to hold the syringe above the surface, extrude a line first, then lay it down where you want. At no time should the syringe tip touch the surface, except to start and stop the line.

Q I can't seem to end my syringe lines properly. They always seem to trail off in long tails. What am I doing wrong?

A To stop a syringe line, stop plunging before you touch down to end the line. Lift your thumb from the plunger right before you're done. Then, touch the syringe line to the surface, and lift straight up.

Q When I tried to use the sgraffito technique with Overlay Paste on a ceramic piece, my design chipped off as I was scratching the clay away. Why did this happen?

A This occurred because the layer of Overlay Paste was too thick. When you dilute the Overlay Paste for sgraffito, it should be the consistency of skim milk, almost translucent. If it's too thick when you apply it, you'll get chipping.

FIRING PROBLEMS

Q I fired a ring with the torch, and it broke as soon as I tried polishing it. What happened?

A This is a really typical sign of underfiring. It's so important to let the piece reach the peach/salmon color before you begin timing the firing cycle. A normally sized ring (approximately 10 g) should be fired at least 2 minutes at the peach/salmon color and allowed to cool. Underfiring results in gaps in the internal structure that weaken the piece. Try turning off the lights in your work area, and wait to get that salmon-colored glow before you start timing.

Q I have a low-fire piece that has a glass cabochon in it. Do I fire it at 1,300 F for 30 minutes, or 1,472 F for 5 minutes?

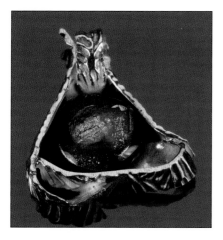

A That all depends on the results you want. At 1,300 F, the glass won't change appearance, and it won't really stick to the metal. You'll have to make sure that the design allows the glass to be captured. At 1,472 F, the glass will be soft enough to begin to change appearance and settle slightly. It also will need to be cooled more slowly, since the metal and glass will have stuck together. If you cool it too quickly, the glass may break away from the metal where they attach.

Q A filigree bead I made over cork clay really distorted during firing. Some of the lines separated and broke. What did I do wrong?

A It sounds like a couple of things are going on. One may be that the syringe lines were too thin. Maybe you had pulled them slightly in laying them over the cork, and they thinned too much. The other problem of distortion and separating could come from improper attachment. Remember, you need to apply paste type to the junction of every line with every other line. If your lines aren't connected prior to firing, they will separate, and the piece will shrink irregularly.

Q **Every time I use the torch to fire, I seem to melt my piece. Why is this happening?**

A One, you're holding your torch too close to the piece during firing. Try turning the lights off in your workroom so you can control the color of the metal. Another thing is to know the signs that you're approaching the melting point.

Your piece will begin to shine, and you may see some sparkles from the surface. Just increase the distance between the piece and the torch.

FINISHING PROBLEMS

Q **I hand polished my piece and then threw it into the tumbler. It came out with tiny indentations. What's wrong?**

A Tumble polishing your piece after you hand polish it is a mistake. Do one or the other, not both. The same is true with hand burnishing. These are all finishing methods that are used separately.

Q The pendant I fired has white inside the bail that I can't get out. How can I fix this?

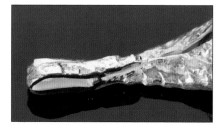

A You have two choices. You can get a stainless steel mini-brush to get inside the bail, or you can leave it. Since the white that results from firing isn't a coating, there's no danger of it "coming off." There's nothing that says you can't leave the inside of the bail white. It provides a contrast, and it will probably all change to silver after a chain slides around inside of it for a while.

Q I tried using liver of sulfur, but all I got was a nasty gray. What went wrong?

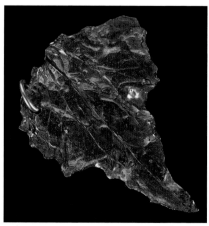

A This could be the result of several issues. First, did you brush and polish your piece? Second, was your liver of sulfur fresh? Third, were your mixing cups clean and free of dirt and detergents? Last, did you dip and rinse quickly enough? The next time you use liver of sulfur, follow these tips, and you should get the desired results.

CHAPTER 10: PROJECTS

Here are four projects — two easy, two hard — to test your mettle as an artist.

Easy projects aren't always simple, but the first two projects are both. Just follow their "recipes" and enjoy!

As for the last two projects, "challenging" is a bit of an understatement. But, they provide an opportunity for you to stretch your wings, and they are designed for you to add your personal touches.

Stamped Bracelet (Easy)

The best thing about this design is its versatility. You can leave the stamped designs plain, you can use a patina (as I did in this instance), or you can go one step further and add some color.

Because the stamped images are nice and deep, polymer clay, resin, glass or acrylic enamels can be added into the recesses after the initial firing and refired or baked according to the manufacturer's instructions.

You even can create a handmade toggle! For an added challenge, try making the stamps using the photopolymer plate technique found on page 60.

No matter what combination you choose, it's a matter of cutting some squares, punching a few holes and stamping the images of choice. What could be easier?

Materials

- 40 g metal clay
- Resealable plastic bag
- 4 stamps
- 12 oval jump rings
- 1 two-piece toggle (or make your own)
- 1.25" x 1.25" polymer clay or cookie cutter
- 1 plastic drinking straw
- Olive oil
- Nonstick work surface
- Roller
- Measuring slats
- Craft knife
- 1 pair of pliers
- Straight and round files
- 600- and 1,200-grit sandpaper
- Firing method of choice
- Drying method of choice
- Liver of sulfur (optional)
- Drying cloth
- Plastic cups
- Polishing cloth
- Wenol metal polish
- Polishing method of choice (burnishing, sanding or tumbling)
- Baking soda

Instructions

1 Oil your hands and tools as appropriate.

2 Roll out the metal clay to a thickness of 1.5 mm, and cut one square.

3 Place the square on an oiled stamp, and roll very gently to make a steady, firm impression.

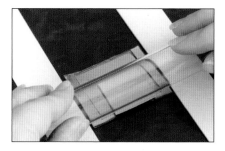

4 Hold the stamp upside down; let gravity assist you as you ease the clay off of the stamp.

5 Place the stamped square right-side up on the work surface. Use the straw to place the connecting holes in two opposite corners.

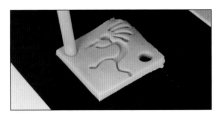

6 Repeat Steps 1 through 5 for the remaining squares.

7 If you plan to make your own two-part toggle, make sure you roll the clay thick enough, since the toggle needs to be strong enough to hold the weight of the bracelet when worn. Use a small coffee stirrer to make the connecting holes in each part. The T-bar needs to be about ½" wider than the diameter of the circle end, and the connecting hole should be centered halfway along the length of the bar.

8 Dry the pieces thoroughly. When they are dry, use files to even the edges and round the corners and holes.

9 Sand the pieces with 600- and 1,200-grit sandpaper. Brush the loose clay into your recycling container.

10 Fire the pieces according to the type of clay used. Allow the pieces to cool completely.

11 Initially polish each piece by burnishing, sanding or tumbling it until shiny.

12 Prepare the liver of sulfur according to your individual preference. Dip each square until it turns black. Rinse well.

13 Use Wenol on the polishing cloth to remove all of the liver of sulfur from each piece, except what is in the recessed design. Buff each piece.

14 Wash each piece with a paste of baking soda and water. Rinse the pieces well, and pat them dry.

15 Use pliers and jump rings to connect the squares and create the bracelet.

16 Connect the round part of the toggle to one end and the T-bar of the toggle to the other. Make sure all of the jump rings are properly closed and secure.

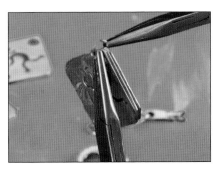

LENTIL BEAD WITH HAND-CARVED DESIGN (EASY)

There's nothing like making something from start to finish. Even the design is your own, and not from a store-bought stamp that thousands of other people also have. Since the eraser or carving pad is soft, you don't need expensive carving tools, either.

MATERIALS

+ 20 g low-fire metal clay
+ Small amount of syringe type
+ Small amount of paste type
+ Resealable plastic bag
+ Nonstick work surface
+ Standard light bulb, any wattage
+ Carving pad or large, soft eraser*
+ Pen
+ Carving tools
+ Roller
+ 1 mm measuring slats
+ Round cookie or clay cutters,
  varying sizes
+ Paintbrush
+ Olive oil
+ Tape
+ Round and flat files
+ 600-grit sandpaper
+ Stainless steel brush
+ Agate burnisher
+ Baking soda
+ Liver of sulfur
+ Plastic cups
+ Drying cloth
+ Electric kiln
+ Piece of fiber blanket
+ Length of chain or silk cord

* **The SpeedyStamp carving pad was
used for this project.**

INSTRUCTIONS

1 Rub a small amount of olive oil on
the round, glass end of the light bulb.

2 Use a pen to draw a design onto the
stamp pad or eraser. Use the carving
tools to carve the marked design.

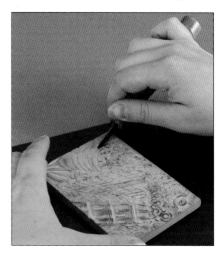

3 Roll out 10 g of metal clay. Stamp it with your design.

4 Use the large cutter to cut a circle shape. Save the extra clay in a resealable plastic bag.

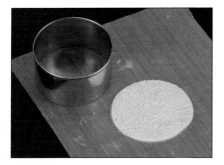

5 Measure ½" from the edge of the circle. Use the small cutter to cut a hole for the cord.

6 Remove the clay from the nonstick surface, and place it on the bulb, gently taping the edges so they lay flat. Prop the bulb against something so it doesn't roll.

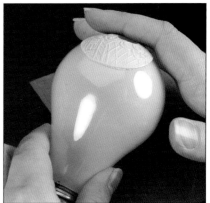

7 Dry the clay. To remove it from the bulb, twist it slightly until the domed shape loosens. Then, turn the bulb over to allow the piece to slide off. Continue to dry the inside of the half bead.

8 Repeat Steps 1 through 7 with the other 10 grams of silver clay. Allow the piece to dry.

9 Use the flat file to shape the inside edges of each of the two halves of the bead so they create a thin, tapered edge and fit well together. Make sure the cord holes line up well.

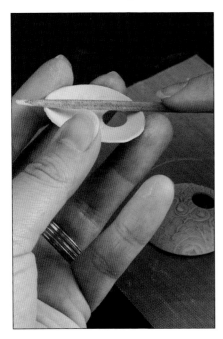

10 Roll out the excess clay, rehydrating it if necessary, and cut a flat, reinforcing ring for each hole. Use a medium-size cutter for the outside, and center the small cutter inside of the first hole.

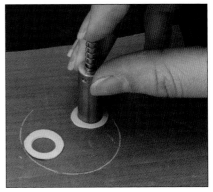

11 Apply a small amount of paste type around the cord hole on each half; apply the reinforcing ring. Paste around the edges to create a solid joint. Repeat for the other half. Allow the piece to dry.

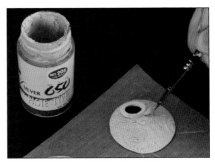

12 Lay a line of syringe type around the inside edge of one of the half beads. Line up the holes, and attach the two halves together; press slightly at the edges. Be careful to avoid pressing too hard on the dome.

13 Reinforce the outside seam with paste type as needed. Allow the piece to dry.

14 File the edges to smooth as necessary. Sand the piece.

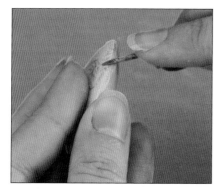

15 Place the bead on fiber blanket. Place it into the kiln.

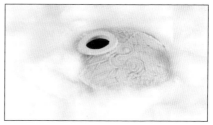

16 Fire the bead at 1,300 F for 30 minutes. Allow it to cool thoroughly.

17 Brush the cooled bead with a stainless steel brush, and use an agate burnisher to highlight the raised portions of the design, the reinforcing rings and the edge of the bead.

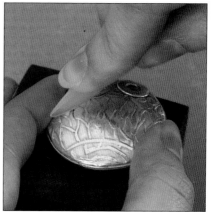

18 Wash the bead with a paste of baking soda and water. Rinse it thoroughly, and allow it to dry.

19 Mix liver of sulfur according to your personal preference. Dip the bead into the solution to produce an attractive array of colors. Rinse the piece well in cold water, and pat it dry.

20 Attach the finished piece to a length of cord or chain.

Box Pendant With Mendhi Design and Garnets (Challenging)

Mendhi designs, which come from India, are beautifully ornate. The box design is Japanese, and the garnets are from Sri Lanka. The color was created with Pébéo's Vitrea 160, but glass enamels or UV resins easily could have been substituted.

When making this piece your own, you can use any gemstone that can be fired with low-fire clays, and the syringed design can be anything you like.

Materials

- 35 g low-fire clay
- 10 g syringe type with small (0.41 mm) nozzle
- Small amount of paste type
- Cork clay
- Resealable plastic bag
- Measuring tape or paper and pencil
- 5 mm to 6 mm fireable cabochons
- 1 drinking straw
- Nonstick work surface
- Scissors
- Small strip of nonstick work surface
- Olive oil
- Roller
- 1 mm measuring slats
- Flat and round files
- Rotary power tool (optional)
- Hand or rotary power drill
- Stainless steel brush
- Adhesive tape
- Fiber blanket
- Magnifier
- Length of silk cord
- 600- and 1,200-grit sandpapers
- Agate burnisher
- Low-fire enamels in sapphire blue, pimento red, sunflower yellow and emerald green*
- Paint brush
- Programmable kiln

* **Note: Pébéo Vitrea 160 products were used for this project**

Instructions

1 Form a piece of cork clay into a box shape that measures approximately 1" wide, 1" high and ½" deep. Dry the cork clay until it is solid and unyielding to the touch.

2 Use a flat file (or rotary power tool, if preferred) to round off the edges of the sides of the box slightly. Brush the filed piece.

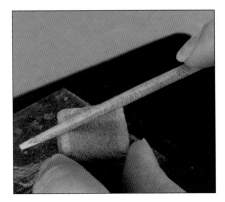

3 Make a mark at the center of one of the long sides of the cork. Use the measuring tape or a long strip of paper to measure the circumference of the cork. Start and stop at the same spot.

4 Roll out 20 g of clay to a thickness of 1 mm. Cut a strip that is 1" wide x the circumference determined in Step 3. Save the remaining clay in a plastic bag.

5 Wet the surface of the cork. Lay the strip of clay around the sides of the form; make sure it's attached to the cork surface. Use syringe and paste type to seal the seam. Dry. File and sand the seam as necessary to make the upper portion of the seam — the part that will show — invisible.

6 Cut the drinking straw into 2 pieces, each 2" long. Apply a small amount of paste on the short sides of the clay-covered cork, and stand one piece of straw against each side, pressing gently to attach. Do not move the pieces, but allow them to air dry.

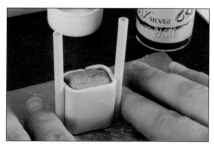

7 Roll out a strip of metal clay that measures ⅝" x 4", or is long enough to lay over the first layer, even with the bottom edge. Wrap this strip completely around the cork and the two straws. This will create the hidden channel for the cord that connects the top and the bottom of the box.

8 Moisten the first layer slightly to help the second layer adhere to the first layer. Start with the same seam line as the first layer so as to have the opposite (front) side of the box clean and smooth. Make sure the sides of the second layer are even and straight. Leave the straws in to dry. Refill the seam if necessary, and file and sand so the seam is invisible.

9 When the piece is dry, gently remove the straws. You should now have two layers of clay, one over the other, with

a ⅜" lip on the top edge. This will be where the lid sits.

10 Before you create the bottom of the box, make sure the bottom edge is level and even. File it as needed. Roll out the clay so it is 1 mm thick and is slightly larger than the bottom of the box. Place the bottom of the dried box over the piece of clay, and trace with a craft knife. Remove and save any extra clay.

11 Apply paste type to the bottom of the box, and carefully line up the edges and attach the two pieces. Return a straw piece to its place in the closed channel on each side and press down; twist very gently to create a hole on each side of the bottom to accommodate the ends of the cords. Leave the box on the nonstick surface to dry.

12 After about 5 minutes, or when the bottom moves freely on the nonstick surface, lay the box on its side and remove the clay made by the straw holes. Allow the bottom of the box to dry completely. File and sand the edges of the bottom; refill with syringe type as necessary.

13 To create the lid, cut a narrow strip of nonstick work surface that is wide enough to reach from the lip to just above the top edge of the cork and long enough to go around the lip's circumference with a little overlap. Attach the work surface snugly. Place a piece of adhesive tape on the nonstick surface, burnish it with a tool to make sure it sticks.

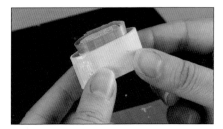

14 Roll a strip of metal clay that is just a hair wider than the nonstick strip and long enough to meet at the back seam. Trim. Attach the seam with syringe and paste types. Dry. Refill, file and sand the seam as necessary.

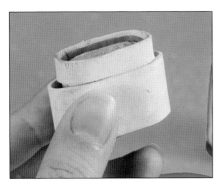

15 Return the straws to fit in the holes in the bottom part. Repeat the process with the straws and second layer of clay over the sides of the lid. Dry, file and sand.

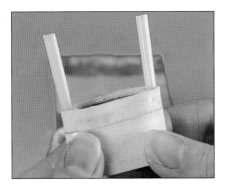

16 Remove the lid from the bottom of the box, and remove the strip of nonstick surface.

17 Check to see that the top edge of the lid is level and even. File and sand it as necessary.

18 Roll out the remaining clay. Create the top in the same manner as the bottom; apply paste type and connect the two pieces.

19 With the lid upside down, place the straws in the channel and press down, making the two holes for the cord.

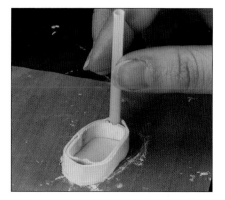

22 With a pencil, draw your design, including placement of stones, syringe work and any other decorations.

20 Allow the lid to dry for 5 minutes, then place the lid on its side and complete the drying process.

21 Trim, file and sand the top edges of the lid. Make sure the lid and box fit well and the lid sits flat and level on the bottom lip. Review your entire piece and refine it as needed.

23 Put the narrow nozzle tip in place on the syringe. Use a magnifier to apply the syringe-type decoration. Even if you are comfortable working with the medium-tipped syringe, you may have to practice working with this narrow tip until you are able to control the lines.

24 If you wish to allow light through the stone, create a hole behind the stone by drilling a hole smaller than the stone with a hand or rotary power drill. Use syringe type to lock the cabochon in place.

25 Complete the remaining decorations, making sure that all of the syringe lines make good and complete contact with the surface. If your syringe lines do not touch, they may pull away or break during firing. Add paste type, if needed, to fill in any gaps.

26 Finally, feel the box for any sharp points or rough spots, and sand those lightly. Check one last time to make sure the top and bottom cord holes line up; refine the piece as needed.

27 Brush all of the dust from the surface decorations, especially from the surface of the gemstones. Remember: Any silver dust left on the stones will contaminate their surfaces.

28 To fire the box, separate the parts. Place the top, right-side up, on the fiber board. Lay the bottom on its side on fiber blanket; place small pieces around it to cushion it well.

29 Fire the box at 1,300 F for 30 minutes in a well-ventilated work area, as the burning cork will create a small amount of smoke. Allow the piece to cool inside the kiln until it reaches room temperature.

30 Remove the box from the kiln, and wash away the cork residue inside of the box. Brush the box with the stainless steel brush until it achieves a matte finish. Make certain the top fits the box properly, and make adjustments as needed.

31 Use the agate burnisher to shine the high spots of the designs. This also will make it easier to remove any stray low-fire enamels that may get on the designs.

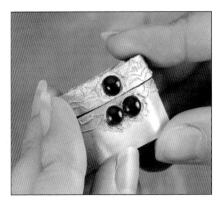

32 Choose which parts of the design to paint. Use your magnifier. Be very careful when you apply the low-fire enamels. These paints are water soluble and can be removed easily with a toothpick.

33 Dry the box for at least 24 hours. If you do not, the colors may develop bubbles during baking.

34 Bake the piece in a toaster oven, kitchen oven or polymer clay oven at 325° F for 40 minutes, and remove it. Thread a silk cord through each side of the box, and knot it to hold the lid and bottom together. Add an adjustable clasp if desired.

Japanese Butterfly Ring (Challenging)

This really could have been any sculptural element on a ring. The butterfly was fashioned in separate pieces, which were dried and then combined. The ring could have been any width or shape; it really is just a landing spot for the butterfly.

Materials

- 20 g low-fire, slow dry metal clay
- Small amount of paste type
- 3 g syringe-type clay with small (0.41 mm) nozzle
- 3" length fine silver wire, 26 gauge
- Ring mandrel with stand
- Ring sizer
- Pencil
- Strip of nonstick work surface
- Adhesive tape
- Stencil or other impressible design
- Paint brush
- Butterfly template
- Roller
- Measuring slats
- Stainless steel brush
- Rotary power tool with various shaping bits
- Small drill bit
- Fiber blanket
- Programmable kiln
- Various polishing discs
- Metal polish
- Round-nose pliers

Instructions

1 Prepare the ring mandrel; see Chapter 6 for detailed instructions. Roll out 10 g of clay to a thickness of 1 mm. Place the stencil or other design on the clay, and roll it in.

2 Remove the stencil. Trim the clay so the ring is approximately 10 mm wide. Wrap the clay around the mandrel, and secure it with syringe and paste type. Dry the piece well.

3 Using the butterfly template, create the butterfly's body shape out of a coil of clay. Allow it dry.

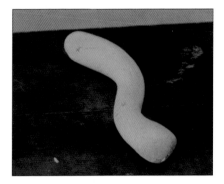

4 Mark the butterfly's body segments with a pencil, and shape them with the power tool.

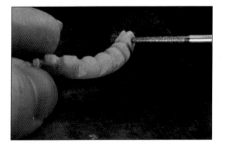

5 Highlight the eyes with syringe and paste type. Dry. Shape the tail.

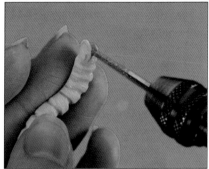

6 Use the small drill bit to drill a hole in the head for the antennae. Fold the wire in half, and cover it with paste type.

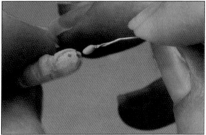

7 Insert the wire into the hole, and secure it with paste type. Dry the piece thoroughly.

8 Create two small triangles, and pinch them together to form the upper, decorative additions to the wings. Repeat with two slightly larger pieces for the lower, decorative wing elements.

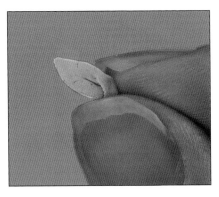

9 Roll out clay for the two main butterfly wings. Cut the pieces into similar shapes per the template.

10 Roll the fiber blanket to approximately the size of the green ware ring; dry the wings on the fiber blanket.

11 Once the wings are dry, use the syringe with the small (0.41 mm) tip to form the upper edge and lattice decoration.

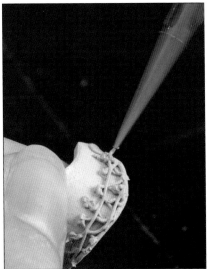

12 Apply Paste Type clay as necessary to secure the lattice work. Use a pointed drill bit to drill small holes in the wings.

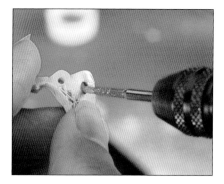

13 File and sand all of the parts prior to assembly.

14 Use syringe type to attach the midpoint of the butterfly's body to the ring top.

15 Apply the main wings to the body as shown. Use syringe and Paste Type as needed.

16 Apply the wing decorative elements, creating a dynamic design.

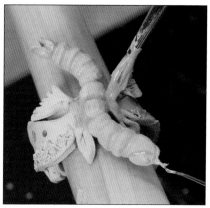

17 Dry the piece thoroughly.

18 Use a generous amount of fiber blanket — especially under the tail and the head — to support the ring upright on a fiber board.

19 Fire the piece at 1,300 F for 30 minutes. Allow it to cool, then brush it with a stainless steel brush.

20 Use the polishing discs in sequence, from coarsest to finest, to create a shine on the flat and high points of the wings, body and ring.

21 Finish with metal polish. Wash and rinse the piece well.

22 Use round-nose pliers to carefully shape the antennae.

Glossary

Alloy — The homogeneous mixture or solid solution of two or more metallic elements or metallic and nonmetallic elements.

Alumina hydrate — A clay-like mineral, composed of aluminum hydroxides, that is used as an abrasive, a catalyst and a refractory for the lining of furnaces that are exposed to intense heat. It is a basic component of ceramics.

Anneal — The process of heating metal to prevent brittleness and make it workable. In jewelry making, precious metals become work-hardened or stressed when they are hammered, forged, rolled or bent (as in fold forming), which makes them brittle.

Appliqué — A decoration or ornament made by cutting pieces of one material and applying them to the surface of another.

Bail — A hoop-like attachment for a pendant that allows it to be worn with a chain.

Ball-peen hammer — A hammer with one spherical, rounded end and one flat end.

Beveled — A surface that has been cut at an angle less than 90 degrees.

Bezel — A ring or band of metal that surrounds a cabochon or faceted stone.

Bisque ware — A ceramic piece that has been fired once, but is unglazed.

Bone dry — A piece that has no moisture remaining.

Brass — An alloy typically composed of 60 percent copper and 40 percent zinc.

Brooch — An ornamental piece of jewelry with a pin and clasp. Brooches are made to be attached to clothing.

Cabochon — A stone that has been cut to create a rounded, convex surface and a flat base. It may be high-domed or almost flat and can be cut in round, oval, square or free-form shapes.

Cameo — A carving traditionally done on shell or stone where the design is carved in relief with a contrasting colored background. Cameo is the opposite of intaglio.

Carat — A unit of metric measurement used for gems. One carat equals 100 points, 200 milligrams or $\frac{1}{5}$ of a gram. It is abbreviated ct.

Ceramics — Inorganic, nonmetallic materials that are typically produced using clays and other minerals from the earth or chemically processed powders.

Cloisonné — A technique where metal filaments are attached to outline a design. Then, these areas are filled with colored enamel and heated at high temperatures to fuse the enamel to the surface.

Corundum — A family of stones composed of crystallized aluminum and oxygen that includes rubies and sapphires. The colors of these stones depend on the oxides present in their composition.

Crown — The part of any faceted gemstone above the girdle.

Culet — The small facet polished across what would otherwise be the sharp point or tip of the pavilion of a faceted stone, especially a round brilliant cut.

Enamel — A substance made of a vitreous pigment of metallic oxide mixed with powdered glass. Enamel is fused to the surface of a metal, like copper, gold, bronze or silver, under very high temperatures.

Engraving — Any pattern design or mark that is cut into a piece of jewelry with a special engraver's tool. Engraving also refers to the process of cutting or carving lines into a surface.

Facet — One of the flat, polished surfaces cut on a gemstone that allows the cut stone to sparkle and reflect light.

Filigree — An intricate, delicate or fanciful ornamentation.

Finding — Any type of construction component used in jewelry making, such as clasps, pins, hooks, tabs, etc.

Fine (pure) silver — Also known as .999 silver. Fine silver contains nothing but the element silver.

Finish — The way the surface of a piece is polished or textured.

Fire scale — A red or purple stain that appears on mixtures of silver and copper, such as sterling silver. At high temperatures, oxygen mixes with the copper to form cuprous oxide and then cupric oxide.

Flange — The protruding rim of a hinge used to hold it in place or attach it to another object.

Gemstone — Any precious or semiprecious stone, rock or mineral.

Girdle — The narrow band around the widest part of a polished or faceted gemstone. The girdle divides the crown and pavilion facets.

Green ware — Dried, unfired ceramic or metal clay. Green ware may be bone dry or leather hard.

High polish — A surface, typically on a piece of jewelry, that has been polished to a mirror-like finish.

Hinge — A jointed or flexible device that allows a part, such as a door or lid, to turn or pivot on a stationary frame.

Inclusion — Any solid, liquid or gaseous foreign body that is enclosed in a mineral or rock.

Intaglio — A carving where a design is cut or carved into stone or metal so that the carving is below the surface of the material. Intaglio is the opposite of cameo.

Karat — The measure of the fineness of gold equal to $\frac{1}{24}$ part. Pure gold is 24-karat gold. Karat usually is abbreviated kt. or k.

Keum Bu or Keum Boo — A jewelry-making technique from Korea where 24k gold foil is fused to silver.

Leather hard — A ceramic or metal clay that contains enough moisture for reworking but too much for firing.

Lost wax casting — An object that is made of wax and coated in clay. When the clay is fired, the wax melts and evaporates or drains away to leave an exact impression of the object in the hardened clay, which is then filled with molten metal.

Mark — A symbol that may indicate the purity of the metal, the maker, the country of manufacture, and/or the date that the piece was assayed or had its design registered. Metal clay may be marked .999. Marks are not officially required in the United States, but they are carried by custom and practice.

Mohs Scale — A measure of a mineral's hardness and its resistance to scratching that was invented by Austrian mineralogist Friedrich Moh. The scale, which ranges from 1 to 10, starts with talc (1) as the softest substance known to man and ends with diamonds (10) as the hardest substance known to man. Most gemstones fall in the range of 6 to 8 on the Mohs Scale.

Mounting — A piece of metal that holds a gem in place.

Nickel silver — A white metal alloy of 70 percent copper, 20 percent zinc and 10 percent nickel. Also called German silver, nickel silver contains no silver. Many people are allergic to nickel, and because of this, the use of nickel silver in jewelry has been outlawed in some countries.

Overfilling — The process of adding more paste than would seem necessary to fill a defect in clay.

Pendant — An ornament or charm that hangs from a cord or chain worn around the neck

Polish — The process of rubbing an object to make it smooth and shiny and reduce the appearance of flaws.

Porcelain — An especially fine kind of pottery that is fired at very high temperatures.

Precious metals — Metals that are valued for their color, malleability and rarity. There are only three precious metals: gold, silver and platinum.

Prong — A thin, pointed, projecting part on a piece of jewelry, such as a prong of a ring setting.

Riveting hammer — A hammer that has one flat end and one narrow, chisel-shaped head used to spread the end of a rivet or eyelet.

Seam — A line, ridge or groove made by fitting, joining, or lapping together two sections along their edges.

Setting — A permanent fixture for a gemstone that is usually made of metal.

Sgraffito — Decoration produced on pottery or ceramics by scratching through one surface to reveal a different color underneath, such as scratching through a thin layer of dried Overlay Paste to reveal the ceramic beneath. When fired, the silver layer is polished.

Shank — The part of a ring that goes around a finger. The shank usually is round or flat, but it may be any shape.

Sintering — Causing metallic particles, such as metallic powder, to form a coherent mass via pressure and by heating the metal without melting it. The process by which metal clay becomes fine silver.

Solder — Any of the various alloys that are fused and applied to a joint between metal objects to unite them without heating the objects to the melting point.

Sterling silver — Silver with a fineness of 925 parts per thousand (92.5 percent) and 75 parts per thousand of copper (7.5 percent copper).

Synthetic gemstones — Gemstones that are produced in a laboratory rather than found in nature. Synthetic gemstones are not "fake," since they have exactly the same chemical characteristics as natural stones, but they are usually flawless and much cheaper than their real counterparts.

Table — The top, horizontal, flat facet on the crown of a faceted gemstone.

Tarnish — Silver and copper sulfide. Tarnish is not an oxide; it occurs when silver is exposed to sulfur-containing compounds.

Toggle — A closure system that is used to secure the ends of bracelets, necklaces and chains. A toggle consists of a bar that slips through a round, square or triangular shape to hold the piece in place.

Vermiculite — A mica-like material that, in expanded form, is used as insulation, in gardening and as a heat-resistant support.

APPENDICES

ART CLAY PRE-FIRED RING SIZE

Art Clay Silver contracts about 8 percent to 9 percent in length when it is fired. The contraction rate depends on the shape and volume of the ring. Prepare the pre-fired ring 1.5 to 2.5 American sizes larger than the intended finished size, depending on the shape and volume. This allows for the contraction of the clay during the firing.

FINGER SIZE	BAND A*	BAND B**	BAND C***
4	5-5.5	5.5-6	6
5	6-6.5	6.5-7	7
6	7-7.5	7.5-8	8
7	8-8.5	8.5-9	9
8	9-9.5	9.5-10	10
9	10-10.5	10.5-11	11
10	11-11.5	11.5-12	12
11	12-12.5	12.5-13	13
12	13-13.5	13.5-14	14
13	14-14.5	14.5-15	15
14	15-15.5	15.5-16	16
15	16-16.5	16.5-17	17
16	17-17.5	17.5-18	18
17	18-18.5	18.5-19	19
18	19-19.5	19.5-20	20

NOTES:

* Band A Band is 3 mm thick
** Band B Band is 1.5 mm thick and/or 10 mm wide
*** Band C Band is thicker and/or wider than A or B

GEMSTONE FIRING GUIDELINES

SPECIES	HARDNESS (MOHS)	SPECIFIC GRAVITY	REFRACTIVE INDEX	DISPERSION	DURABILITY
Alabaster	1-1.5	2.2-2.4	1.52	medium-high	low
Alexandrite*	8	3.68-3.78	1.75	low	high
Amber	2.5	1.03-1.1	1.54	none	low
Apatite*	5	3.16-3.22	1.64-1.65	low	medium
Aquamarine	7.75	2.68-2.7	1.57-1.575	low	high
Azurite	3.5	3.8	1.48-1.65	none	low
Beryl*	7.75	2.70	1.58	low	high
Cat's Eye*	8	2.68-3.79	1.54-1.75	low	high
Chalcedony	7	2.65	1.55	low	high
Chrysoberyl*	8.5	3.71	1.75	low	high
Corundum*	9	—	—	low	high
Diamond	10	3.52	2.42	high	high
Emerald*	7.75	2.66-2.78	1.56	low	high
Epidote	6	3.25-3.49	1.73-1.76	medium-high	high
Feldspar**	6-6.5	—	—	low	medium
Garnet**	7.5	2.7-4.16	1.74-1.89	medium-high	high
Gypsum	1-1.5	2.3	1.53	medium-high	low
Hematite**	5.5-6.5	4.95-5.3	2.94-3.22	none	high
Jade	6.5-7	3.3-3.38	1.68	none	high
Jadite	7	3.33	1.66	none	high
Jet	3.5	1.1-1.4	1.64-1.68	none	low
Kunzite	7	3.13-3.31	1.66-1.68	medium	low
Labradorite**	6	2.7-2.72	1.52	medium	medium
Lapis Lazuli	5	2.76-2.94	1.5	none	medium
Malachite	3-4	3.7-4	1.87-1.98	none	low
Marble	3	2.71	1.48-1.65	none	low

GEMSTONE FIRING GUIDELINES CONTINUED

SPECIES	HARDNESS (MOHS)	SPECIFIC GRAVITY	REFRACTIVE INDEX	DISPERSION	DURABILITY
Moonstone**	6	2.5-2.55	1.52-1.54	low	high
Nephrite	6.5	2.96	1.62	none	high
Obsidian**	6	2.33-2.6	1.48-1.51	high	medium
Olivine	6	3.3-3.5	1.65	medium	high
Opal	6	1.97-2.2	1.45	none	low
Peridot**	6.5	3.34	1.68	low	medium
Quartz	7	2.65	1.55	low	high
Rodonite	5	3.53	1.73-1.74	none	medium
Ruby*	9	4	1.77	low	high
Sapphire	9	4	1.77	low	high
Serpentine	3.5	2.5-2.7	1.57	low	low
Sodalite	5	2.13-2.29	1.483	low	medium
Spectrolite**	6	2.7-2.72	1.52	low	medium
Sphene	5	3.45-3.56	1.95-2.05	high	medium
Spinel*	8	3.6	1.72	low	high
Spodumene	7	3.18	1.66	low	low
Steatite	1-1.5	2.7-2.8	—	none	low
Topaz	8	3.54	1.63	low	medium
Tourmaline	7	3.06	1.63	low	high
Turquoise	5	2.6-2.8	1.61-1.65	none	medium
Zircon	7	4.02	1.81	high	high

NOTES:
* Can be fired at 1,472 F for 30 minutes with ACS Standard Series
** Can successfully be fired using 650/1200 Low-Fire Series

Art Clay Drying Times

ART CLAY TYPE*	HOT AIR DRYER**	COOKING PLATE	KILN	AIR DRY
ACS 650	More than 10 minutes	More than 10 minutes at 150 C/302 F	More than 10 minutes at 150 C/302 F	More than 24 hours
ACS 650 Slow Dry	More than 45 minutes	More than 20 minutes at 150 to180 C/ 302 to 356 F	More than 20 minutes at 150 to 180 C/ 302 to 356 F	Not recommended
Overlay Silver Paste	More than 10 minutes	More than 10 minutes at 100 C/212 F	More than 10 minutes at 100 C/212 F	More than 60 minutes
ACS Basic	More than 15 minutes	More than 20 minutes at 150 C/320F	More than 20 minutes at 150 C/320F	More than 24 hours
ACS Basic Slow Dry	More than 45 minutes	More than 20 minutes at 150 to 180 C/ 302 to 356 F	More than 20 minutes at 150 to 180 C/ 302 to 356 F	Not recommended
ACS Paper Type	No need to dry	No need to dry	No need to dry	No need to dry
ACS Oil Paste	More than 30 minutes	More than 30 minutes at 100 C/212 F	More than 30 minutes at 100 C/212 F	More than 24 hours
AC Gold Clay Type	More than 15 minutes	More than 10 minutes at 150 C/320 F	More than 10 minutes at 150 C/320 F	More than 24 hours
AC Gold Paste Type (Undiluted)	More than 5 minutes	Not recommended	Not recommended	More than 15 minutes
AC Gold Paste Type (Diluted)	Depends on the medium amount	Not recommended	Not recommended	NO

NOTES:

* The test pieces used for this chart are in 5 g clay volume.
** A 1,200-watt hot air dryer was used 3 cm to 4 cm away from the drying pieces

Art Clay Holding Times and Kiln Firing Temperatures
650 C/1,202 F to 780 C/1,436 F

CLAY TYPE	650 C OR 1,202 F	700 C OR 1,292 F	750 C OR 1,382 F	780 C OR 1,436 F
ACS 650	30 minutes	15 minutes	10 minutes	5 minutes
ACS 650 Slow Dry	30 minutes	15 minutes	10 minutes	5 minutes
Overlay Silver Paste	30 minutes	15 minutes	10 minutes	5 minutes
ACS Basic	—	—	—	—
ACS Basic Slow Dry	—	—	—	—
ACS Paper Type	—	—	—	—
ACS Oil Paste	—	—	—	—
ACG Clay Type	—	—	—	—
ACG Paste Type on fired ACS	500 C/932 F to 800 C/1,472 F; hold 5 minutes	500 C/932 F to 800 C/1,472 F; hold 5 minutes	500 C/932 F to 800 C/1,472 F; hold 5 minutes	500 C/932 F to 800 C/1,472 F; hold 5 minutes
ACG Paste Type on Porcelain Surface	Cold kiln; 800 C/1,472 F; switch off; under 100 C/212 F to take out	Cold kiln; 800 C/1,472 F; switch off; under 100 C/212 F to take out	Cold kiln; 800 C/1,472 F; switch off; under 100 C/212 F to take out	Cold kiln; 800 C/1,472 F; switch off; under 100 C/212 F to take out
ACG Paste Type on Glass Surface	Cold kiln; 800 C/1,472 F; hold 5 minutes; crash cool to 600 C; close kiln door; natural cool to take out	Cold kiln; 800 C/1,472 F; hold 5 minutes; crash cool to 600 C; close kiln door; natural cool to take out	Cold kiln; 800 C/1,472 F; hold 5 minutes; crash cool to 600 C; close kiln door; natural cool to take out	Cold kiln; 800 C/1,472 F; hold 5 minutes; crash cool to 600 C; close kiln door; natural cool to take out

NOTES:

Test pieces used for this chart are in 5 g clay volume.

* Holding time; fire from cold kiln

Art Clay Holding Times and Kiln Firing Temperatures
800 C/1,472 F to 900 C/1,814 F

CLAY TYPE	800 C OR 1,472 F	850 C OR 1,562 F	870 C OR 1,598 F	900 C OR 1,814 F
ACS 650	5 minutes	—	—	—
ACS 650 Slow Dry	5 minutes	—	—	—
Overlay Silver Paste*	0 minutes	—	—	—
ACS Basic	30 minutes	20 minutes	10 minutes	—
ACS Basic Slow Dry	30 minutes	20 minutes	10 minutes	—
ACS Paper Type*	30 minutes	20 minutes	—	—
ACS Oil Paste	30 minutes	10 minutes	—	—
ACG Clay Type	—	—	—	60 minutes
ACG Paste Type on fired ACS	500 C/932 F to 800 C/1,472 F; hold 5 minutes	500 C/932 F to 800 C/1,472 F; hold 5 minutes	500 C/932 F to 800 C/1,472 F; hold 5 minutes	500 C/932 F to 800 C/1,472 F; hold 5 minutes
ACG Paste Type on Porcelain Surface	Cold kiln; 800 C/1,472 F; switch off; under 100 C/212 F to take out	Cold kiln; 800 C/1,472 F; switch off; under 100 C/212 F to take out	Cold kiln; 800 C/1,472 F; switch off; under 100 C/212 F to take out	Cold kiln; 800 C/1,472 F; switch off; under 100 C/212 F to take out
ACG Paste Type on Glass Surface	Cold kiln; 800 C/1,472 F; hold 5 minutes; crash cool to 600 C; close kiln door; natural cool to take out	Cold kiln; 800 C/1,472 F; hold 5 minutes; crash cool to 600 C; close kiln door; natural cool to take out	Cold kiln; 800 C/1,472 F; hold 5 minutes; crash cool to 600 C; close kiln door; natural cool to take out	Cold kiln; 800 C/1,472 F; hold 5 minutes; crash cool to 600 C; close kiln door; natural cool to take out

NOTES:

Test pieces used for this chart are in 5 g clay volume

* Holding time; fire from cold kiln

Alternative Methods To Firing For Art Clay Series

CLAY TYPE	STOVE TOP	GAS TORCH
ACS 650	Yes	Yes
ACS 650 Slow Dry	Yes	Yes
Overlay Silver Paste	When used without glass or ceramics	When used without glass or ceramics
ACS Basic	Yes	Yes
ACS Basic Slow Dry	Yes	Yes
ACS Paper Type	Small pieces (i.e. appliqué on green ware)	Small pieces (i.e. appliqué on green ware)
ACS Oil Paste	Small pieces (i.e. flat bezel wire seams)	Small pieces (i.e. flat bezel wire seams)
ACG Clay Type	No	Only as paste form on already-fired silver
ACG Paste Type Application on Fired ACS	Yes	No
ACG Paste Type Application on Porcelain Surface	No	No
ACG Paste Type Application on Glass Surface	No	No

NOTE:

Test pieces used for this chart are in 5 g clay volume.

Contributors

ART CLAY WORLD USA, INC.
4535 Southwest Highway
Oak Lawn, IL 60453
Phone: 866-381-0100
Fax: 708-636-5408
E-mail: info@artclayworld.com
International e-mail: overseas@artclay.co.jp
Web: www.artclayworld.com

CHASE HOLDING COMPANY, INC.
2057 Goodyear Ave., Suite F
Ventura, CA 93003
Phone: 805-339-6300
Web: www.andale.com

KRAUSE PUBLICATIONS
700 E. State St.
Iola, WI 54990
Phone: 888-457-2873
Web: www.krausebooks.com

PARAGON INDUSTRIES
2011 South Town East Blvd.
Mesquite, TX 75149-1122
Phone: 800-876-4328
E-mail: info@paragonweb.com
Web: www.paragonweb.com

PEACOCK INDUSTRIES
225 Cash St.
Jacksonville, TX 75766
Phone: 800-388-2001

PINZART
10945 State Bridge Road
Suite 401-277
Alpharetta, GA 30022
Phone: 888-335-9884 or 770-752-1641
Fax: 509-352-1009
Web: www.pinzart.com

PRAIRIE STAINED GLASS
587 Sargent Ave.
Winnipeg, Manitoba, Canada R3B1W6
Phone: 204-783-1117
Fax: 204-783-3223
E-mail: psg@mts.net
Web: www.prairiestainedglass.mb.ca

THE CONTENTI COMPANY
123 Stewart St.
Providence, RI 02903
Phone: 401-421-4040
Web: www.contenti.com

Additional Resources
Art Clay Distributors in North America

CANADA

ALBERTA
ART CLAY CANADA
Phone: 780-430-4353
Web: spiritoftherock.ca

MANITOBA
PRAIRIE STAINED GLASS LTD.
Phone: 204-783-1117
Web: www.prairiestainedglass.mb.ca

ONTARIO
BEADFX INC.
Phone: 877-473-2323
Web: www.beadfx.com

OTTAWA
RAINBOW MINERALS
Phone: 613-733-8440
Web: www.rainbowminerals.com

UNITED STATES

ALABAMA
THE BEAD BIZ LLC
Phone: 205-621-2426
Web: thebeadbiz.com

CALIFORNIA
AM COLLECTION
Phone: 925-256-8684
Web: www.amcollection.biz

BEADS AND ROCKS
Phone: 510-981-1947
www.beadsandrocks.com

BELLE MELANGE
Phone: 760-942-3911
Web: www.louiseduhamel.com

BREA BEAD WORKS
Phone: 714-671-9976
Web: www.breabeadworks.com

DESIGNS BY JONNA
Phone: 858-456-5257
E-mail: jonnaf@san.rr.com

MERMAID SONG
Phone: 805-402-4116
E-mail: jenik@value.net

NASCO
Phone: 800-558-9595
Web: www.eNASCO.com

THE BEADIAK
Phone: 818-597-8020
Web: www.beadiak.com

COLORADO
NATURAL ATTRACTIONS JEWELRY
Phone: 970-255-1667
Web: www.najewelry.com

CONNECTICUT
ART & SOUL GALLERY
Phone: 860-688-4333
E-mail: lisel33@sbcglobal.net

FLORIDA
ATLANTIC POTTERY SUPPLY
Phone: 904-339-0014
Web: www.atlanticpotterysupply.com

CRYSTAL CREATIONS
Phone: 561-649-9909
E-mail: crystalcreations@msn.com

GIFTS OF AVALON
Phone: 352-379-1272
Web: www.giftsofavalon.com

PEARL – FINE ART SUPPLIES
Phone: 800-451-7327
Web: www.pearlpaint.com

GEORGIA
PINZART
Phone: 888-335-9884
Web: www.pinzart.com

HAWAII
BEAD IT!
Phone: 800-280-2323
Web: www.ibeads.com

ILLINOIS
ALEXANDER BEADS
Phone: 618-462-9100
Web: www.alexanderbeads.com

DICK BLICK ART MATERIALS
Phone: 800-828-4548
Web: www.dickblick.com

ED HOY'S INTERNATIONAL
Phone: 800-323-5668
Web: www.edhoy.com

INDIANA
ABR IMAGERY
Phone: 812-339-8947
Web: www.abrimagery.com

MARYLAND
CALDRON CRAFTS
Phone: 410-744-2155
Web: www.caldroncrafts.com

MICHIGAN
DELPHI STAINED GLASS
Phone: 800-248-2048
Web: ww.delphiglass.com

MUNRO CRAFTS
Phone: 248-544-1590
Web: www.munrocrafts.com

NOTIONS MARKETING
Phone: 616-243-8424
Web: www.notions-marketing.com

MINNESOTA
VEBROD GEM GALLERY
Phone: 952-595-8338
Web: www.vgems.net

NEVADA
BEADLOVER
Phone: 702-499-0272
Web: www.beadlover.com

NEW JERSEY
CERAMIC SUPPLY
Phone: 800-723-7264
Web: www.7ceramic.com

UTRECHT ART SUPPLIES
Phone: 609-409-8001
Web: www.utrechtart.com

NEW MEXICO
ART CLAY NATION
Phone: 505-332-9245
Web: www.artclaynation.com

NEW MEXICO CLAY
Phone: 800-781-2529
Web: www.nmclay.com

NEW YORK
ERIN'S BEADS
Phone: 516-997-5580
Web: www.erinsbeads.com

I DREAM OF BEADING LTD.
Phone: 845-452-7611
Web: www.idreamofbeading.com

NORTH CAROLINA
BEDIZEN ORNAMENTS INC.
Phone: 919-834-8634
Web: www.ornamentea.com

NORTH DAKOTA
URBAN GIRL INC.
Phone: 701-667-7300
Web: www.urbangirlonline.com

OREGON
FIRE MOUNTAIN GEMS AND BEADS
Phone: 800-355-2137
Web: www.firemountaingems.com

PENNSYLVANIA
ARGENTO DESIGNS
Phone: 215-519-0295
E-mail: kasticker@aol.com

PUERTO RICO
YOU CAN DO IT INC.
Phone: 787-502-4534
Web: www.pedrerias.com

RHODE ISLAND
THE CONTENTI CO.
Phone: 401-421-4040
Web: www.contenti.com

SOUTH CAROLINA
CLAY-KING.COM INC.
Phone: 864-585-6014
Web: www.clay-king.com

TEXAS
BEADAHOLIQUE BEAD SHOP
Phone: 281-257-0510
Web: www.beadoholique.com

BLY ENTERPRISES INC.
Phone: 972-264-6573
E-mail: salliannebly@yahoo.com

PMC SUPPLY
Phone: 800-388-2001
Web: www.artclaysupply.com

VIRGINIA
BEADS AND ROCKS
Phone: 757-428-9824
Web: www.beadsandrocks.com

WASHINGTON
FRANTZ ART GLASS & SUPPLY
Phone: 800-839-6712
Web: www.frantzartglass.com

RINGS AND THINGS
Phone: 800-366-2156
Web: www.rings-things.com

SEATTLE POTTERY SUPPLY INC.
Phone: 206-587-0373
Web: www.seattlepotterysupply.com

WISCONSIN
NASCO
Phone: 800-558-9595
Web: www.eNASCO.com

INTERNATIONAL

ARGENTINA
ART CLAY WORLD, ARGENTINA
Web: www.veahcolor.com.ar

AUSTRALIA
SILVERLAB PTY. LTD.
Web: www.silverlab.com.au

AUSTRIA, FRANCE AND SWITZERLAND
CREATIVE GLASS - MHS AG
Web: www.creative-glass.com

BELGIUM, NETHERLANDS AND LUXEMBOURG
ART CLAY WORLD BENELUX
Web: www.artclaysilver.nl

BRAZIL
ART CLAY WORLD BRASIL-JOIA UNICALTDA
Web: www.artclay.com.br

CHILE
ART CLAY WORLD, CHILE
Web: www.artclay.cl

CHINA
BEIJING JIDUO BAOSHI YISHUPIN YAOXIAN ZEREN GONGSI
Web: www.artclay.com.cn/index

CZECH REPUBLIC
ART CLAY WORLD, CZECH
Web: www.atelierstribra.cz

DENMARK
RAVSTEDHUS APS
Web: www.ravstedhus.dk

ENGLAND
ART CLAY WORLD UK
Web: artclayworld.org.uk

GERMANY
ART CLAY WORLD GERMANY
Web: www.efco.de

HONG KONG, MACAU, GUANG DONG
SILVER CREATION
Web: www.silverclaycreation.com

HUNGARY
GLASS DESIGN KFT
Web: www.glass-design.hu/

ICELAND
ART CLAY WORLD, ICELAND
Web: www.handverkshusid.is

ISRAEL
ART CLAY WORLD, ISRAEL
Web: www.art-clay.co.il

ITALY, GREECE, PORTUGAL AND SPAIN
HOBBYLAND S.R.L.
Web: www.hobbyland.it

LATVIA, LITHUANIA, ESTONIA
ART CLAY WORLD, LATVIA
E-mail: delica@e-teliamtc.lv

KOREA
ART CLAY WORLD CO., LTD. KOREA
Web: www.artclay.co.kr

NEW ZEALAND
ART CLAY WORLD NEW ZEALAND LTD.
Web: www.artclaynz.co.nz

NORWAY AND FINLAND
ART CLAY WORLD, SCANDINAVIA
Web: www.artclayworldscandinavia.no

POLAND
ART CLAY STUDIO
Web: www.planetart.pl

SINGAPORE, THAILAND, MALAYSIA, INDONESIA
ART CLAY SILVER AND GOLD SINGAPORE
Web: www.beadhub.com

SLOVENIA
PROMETEJ ART & HOBBY D.O.O.
Web: www.atelierstribra.cz

SOUTH AFRICA
ART CLAY SILVER SOUTH AFRICA
Web: www.artclaysilversa.com

SWEDEN
ART CLAY WORLD, SCANDINAVIA
E-mail: info@sargenta.se

TAIWAN
ART CLAY WORLD CO., LTD. TAIWAN
Web: www.hobbydiy.com.tw

THAILAND
VOICE (THAILAND) CO., LTD.
Web: www.homepage.mac.com/voicet/Menu4.html

TURKEY
ART CLAY WORLD, TURKEY
Web: www.odakhobi.com

UKRAINE
ART CLAY WORLD, UKRAINE
Web: www.artclay.com.ua

VENEZUELA
REPRESENTACIONES ARCAM C,A.
Web: www.grupoarcam.com

ALL OTHER COUNTRIES
AIDA CHEMICAL INDUSTRIES CO., LTD.
6-28-3 Minami-cho Fuchu City
Tokyo, Japan 183-0026
Phone: +81-42-366-8751
Fax: +81-42-366-8707
E-mail: overseas@artclay.co.jp
Web site: www.artclay.co.jp

INDEX

MORE EXPERT REFERENCES FOR CREATING MAGNIFICENT METAL

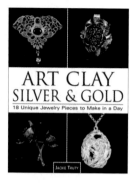

Art Clay Silver & Gold
18 Unique Jewelry Pieces to Make in a Day
by Jackie Truty

An all-in-one resource for Art Clay, this easy to follow book features 18 great jewelry projects for all skill levels. Nearly 200 color photos and illustrations guide readers through each fantastic creation from start to finish.

Softcover w/flaps • 8¼ x 10⅞ • 128 pages
150+ color photos, illus.
Item# OJAC • $21.99

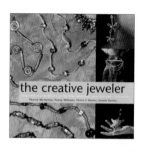

The Creative Jeweler
Inspirational Projects Using Semi-precious and Everyday Materials
by Sharon McSwiney, Penny Williams, Clare C. Davies, Jennie Davies

Whether elegant, fun, classic, or modern, readers are sure to find inspiration from the more than 50 step-by-step projects, including pins, brooches, bangles, bracelets, necklaces, and earrings.

Softcover • 8¾ x 8¾ • 160 pages
200 color photos
Item# CRJE • $21.95

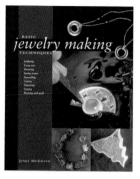

Basic Jewelry Making Techniques
by Jinks McGrath

Provides detailed instructions and illustrations for featured projects using silver, wood, acrylic, and more that utilize all modern jewelry-making techniques-instant reference tables are included for conversion formulas and melting point temperatures.

Softcover W/Flaps • 8½ x 11 • 112 pages
125 color photos
Item# JMT • $24.99

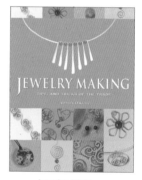

Jewelry Making
Tips and Tricks of the Trade
by Stephen O'Keeffe

Making jewelry at a professional level has never been so simple. Every technique is photographed step-by-step with explanations of common pitfalls and how to avoid them. Features more than 50 original projects.

Softcover • 8¼ x 10⅞ • 128 pages
250+ color photos
Item# JMCH • $24.99

First Steps in Enameling
by Jinks McGrath

Doubling as a beginner's manual and an essential reference guide, this book mixes step-by-step instructions with inspiration in 20 flexible projects encouraging readers to practice skills and be inventive.

Softcover w/flaps • 8½ x 11 • 96 pages
120 color photos
Item# FSE • $24.99